Fort Snelling at Bdote

A BRIEF HISTORY
NEWLY ANNOTATED

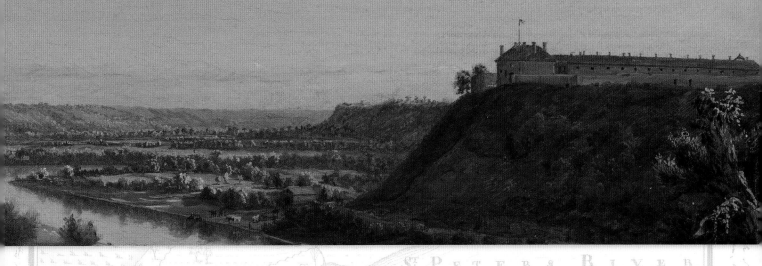

PETER DeCARLO

MINNESOTA
HISTORICAL
SOCIETY PRESS

At Bdote in the late 1840s Ḣaḣa Wakpa (the Mississippi River) is at right; Mni Sota Wakpa (the Minnesota River) enters it below the fort, around Wita Taŋka (Pike Island). The St. Peters Indian Agency is to the left of the fort. The homestead in the foreground is likely owned by a trader or resident of Mendota. The figure appears to be a Dakota person. Watercolor painting by Seth Eastman, 1846–48.

Two great rivers come together in the center of North America, at what are now the Twin Cities of Minneapolis and St. Paul, Minnesota. The Mississippi and Minnesota rivers drain huge portions of the state, and for millennia they were the region's highways, bringing people together at their confluence. An Indigenous people of this region, the Dakota, call the place where the Minnesota enters the Mississippi Bdote (Mdote), which means "where two waters come together," and it is sacred, surrounded by spiritual sites and the graves of relatives.

Fort Snelling, the limestone fortress built by US soldiers at Bdote in the 1820s, is considered by many people to be the "birthplace of Minnesota," a symbol of patriotism and pioneer spirit, a place to celebrate the armed forces and honor veterans. But in the Indigenous history of Bdote, those very qualities can represent invasion, dispossession, and destruction.

There are many other stories about this place that touch the heart of American history. For nearly two hundred years, during the fur trade era, cultures blended to form a unique borderland society. Dakota and Ojibwe leaders met with US officials at Bdote and important treaties were signed there. After the US–Dakota War of 1862, about sixteen hundred Dakota, mostly women, children, and elders, were held through the winter in a concentration camp below the fort. US Army officers enslaved African Americans at the confluence for nearly three decades. Dred and Harriet Robinson Scott met and married at Bdote and fought for their freedom; they based their US Supreme Court case on having been enslaved at Fort Snelling, in a free territory. African Americans also made their mark on Bdote as fur traders, cultural

intermediaries, freedmen, and Buffalo Soldiers sent to fight Indigenous people in the North American West. From the Spanish-American War through World Wars I and II, hundreds of thousands of men and women passed through the Fort Snelling military reservation as they were sent off to war. Many of these soldiers are buried in the nearby Fort Snelling National Cemetery. The fort holds special meaning for Japanese American veterans of World War II. When the loyalty of US citizens of Japanese ancestry was questioned, thousands volunteered and trained at the Fort Snelling Military Intelligence Service Language School.

History continues to be made at Bdote. The reconstruction of the military post as Historic Fort Snelling in the 1960s and '70s can teach us lessons about public memory, commemoration, and the practice of truth telling. Today, Bdote is covered with federally operated buildings, urban development, a national cemetery, a state park, highways, and the state of Minnesota's first national landmark, which encompasses Historic Fort Snelling and the area around it. Bdote is still a place through which diverse peoples travel. Servicemen and -women are still

As a Dakota person who comes from the villages closest to Fort Snelling, this place means *who I am*. After the 1862 Dakota War, our grandfather Cloud Man died in the concentration camp and my family was exiled from Minnesota. Fort Snelling represents pain and suffering to my people. But this is where my family found the land that provided for them, found the stories that sustained their families, found the beauty. In one sense, I came to life as the person I am because I returned to this place.

—Syd Beane, educator, activist, filmmaker (Mdewakantonwan/ Wahpetonwan Dakota, French, English)

I came to Fort Snelling on Christmas Day, 1945, to be part of the Military Intelligence Service Language School, where they trained linguists in Japanese. It was five below zero; it was Minnesota's welcome to people from Hawaii. People were so gracious and kind to us. People looked upon you as being a US army soldier, an American citizen. This is what has kept me here all these years, despite the cold.

—Edwin "Bud" Nakasone, veteran

My ancestors were a part of the history that ended slavery, and it happened here, at Fort Snelling. It is an absolute joy to be able to say, *I'm in the place where they walked.* You're not going to get that in a history book. You can read about it, but you have to really be there, if you can, to see it.

—Lynne Jackson, great-great-granddaughter of Dred and Harriet Scott

The Power of Place

The history of this place carries all the weight of the condition of humanity, and I continually find myself questioning its *meanings*. I sometimes go in circles on the ethical dilemmas, never quite sorting out the answers—but wanting to try harder each time around the next bend. There is enough angst here to make you want to run as far away as you can get, but I find that I have a simultaneous obsession for telling everyone who will listen all the stories and lessons this place has to offer.

—Jeff Boorom, program manager, Historic Fort Snelling

Fort Snelling to me is like this living, breathing artifact. If you look at the fort as an artifact, then it's our responsibility to look at all the nuances of that artifact. It's not just one narrative that's important. It's all the narratives that are important.

—Alisha Volante, activist and PhD candidate, University of Minnesota

The first thing that people should know when they enter that space is that this is Dakota land. They should acknowledge that there's a concentration camp connected to Fort Snelling. Juxtaposed right next to that patriotism and that honor and that pride in this place's military history is despair, a horrible history. Minnesotans can only benefit by understanding and accepting and acknowledging all these complicated histories.

—Amber Annis, PhD candidate, University of Minnesota (Cheyenne River Sioux Tribe)

deployed from Fort Snelling. The nearby international airport welcomes thousands of immigrants each year. Dakota sacred sites still exist and continue to be honored by Dakota people and others who understand.

Historic Fort Snelling stands on sacred land. The fort's diverse history rests on the colonization of that land and its peoples. In listening to *all* of the stories of this place, Minnesotans can learn more about who we are, for the place where the rivers come together is part of our collective identity.

Oceti Śakowiŋ and Bdote Mni Sota

The first ways of knowing about Bdote are taught by those who have lived there the longest, the Dakota.

The Dakota people are part of the Oceti Śakowiŋ, or Seven Council Fires, commonly called the Sioux, or Great Sioux Nation. Dakota, Nakota, and Lakota comprise the three major divisions of the Oceti Śakowiŋ.

Among the Oceti Śakowiŋ, as with virtually every other people, there are many stories and beliefs. These traditions tell the Oyate (the People, the Nation) how they came to be, how all land is sacred, and what their responsibilities are to one another and to the land. Some creation stories involve powerful spirits, and many teach lessons.[1]

While there is no single creation story that compels belief, one account is widely held in this region. The spirits of the people came down from Caŋku Wanaġi, "the spirit road," made up of the stars of the Milky Way, and when they arrived on earth, the Creator shaped the first people from the clay of Maka Ina, "mother earth." The people were the Oceti Śakowiŋ, a society that reflected their cosmic origin.

The center of Dakota homeland is Mni Sota Makoce (Minnesota), "the land where the waters reflect the clouds." Many Dakota people believe that they and the Oyate originated at the confluence of the Mni Sota Wakpa (Minnesota) and Ħaħa Wakpa (Mississippi) rivers. The mouth of Mni Sota Wakpa is called Bdote Mni Sota, and the district around it is generally called Bdote. At the heart of Bdote is Wita Taŋka (Pike Island), which some believe is the center of Dakota creation, where people were first made. At the confluence and everywhere, mni—water—is sacred. All water was pure at the time of creation and, like the land, was part of the people.[2]

The area around Bdote encompasses several Dakota places of power, sacred sites. North of the confluence are Owamniyomni (St. Anthony Falls) and Mniħaħa (Minnehaha Falls). A powerful water-being, or Uŋkteħi,

The Oceti Śakowiŋ

THE DAKOTA INCLUDE four of the Oceti Śakowiŋ's seven council fires: the Bdewakaŋtuŋwaŋ (the spiritual people who live by the water), the Waħpetuŋwaŋ (the people who live in the forest), the Sisituŋwaŋ (the medicine people who live by the water), and the Waħpekute (the warriors who protect the medicine people and could shoot from among the leaves).

The Nakota, also known as the western Dakota, traveled west to present-day North and South Dakota. They include the Ihaŋktuŋwaŋ (the people who live at the edge of the great forest) and the Ihaŋktuŋwaŋna (those scattered at the edge of the forest). Further west in what today is South Dakota and Montana live the Lakota, who made up the seventh council fire. They are called the Tituŋwaŋ (dwellers of the plains). These seven groups are the Oyate—the People, the Nation—related by blood, language, beliefs, and customs.[1] ◖

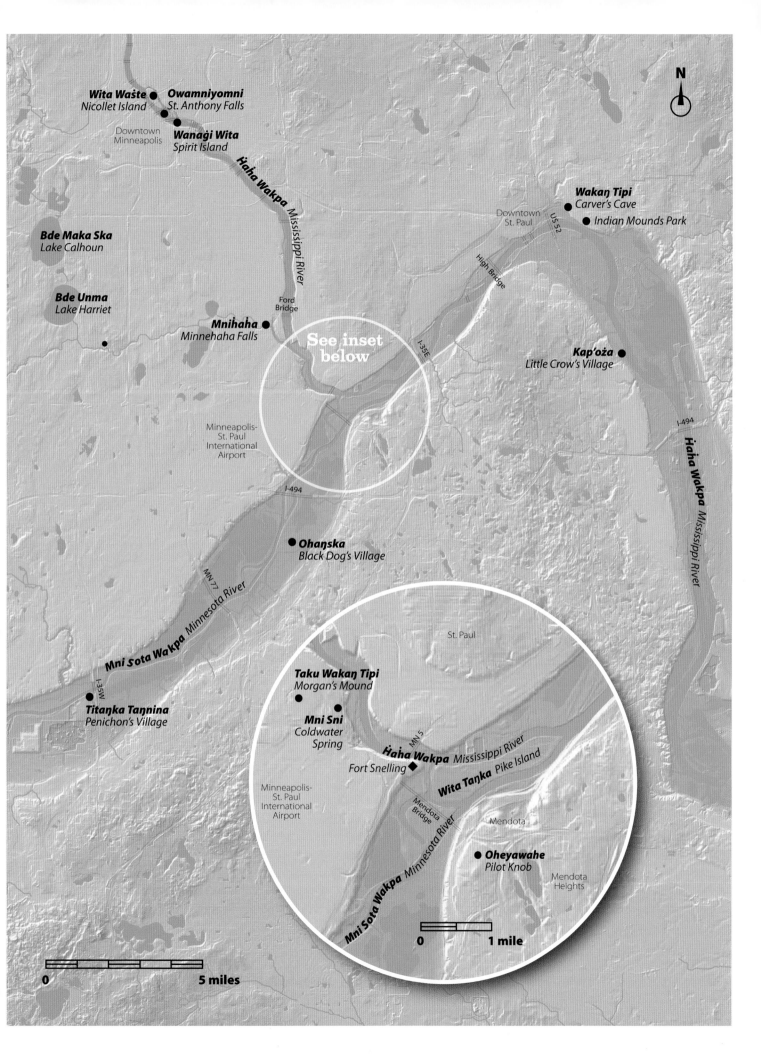

N

Wita Wašte
Nicollet Island

Owamniyomni
St. Anthony Falls

Downtown
Minneapolis

Wanaġi Wita
Spirit Island

Ḣaḣa Wakpa Mississippi River

Wakaŋ Tipi
Carver's Cave

Downtown
St. Paul

US 52

● Indian Mounds Park

High Bridge

Bde Maka Ska
Lake Calhoun

Bde Unma
Lake Harriet

I-35E

Kap'oża
Little Crow's Village

Mniḣaḣa
Minnehaha Falls

Ford
Bridge

See inset
below

I-494

Ḣaḣa Wakpa Mississippi River

Minneapolis-
St. Paul
International
Airport

I-494

● **Ohaŋska**
Black Dog's Village

MN 77

Mni Sota Wakpa Minnesota River

I-35W

Titaŋka Taŋnina
Penichon's Village

St. Paul

Taku Wakaŋ Tipi
Morgan's Mound

Mni Sni
Coldwater
Spring

MN 5

Ḣaḣa Wakpa Mississippi River

Fort Snelling ◆

Wita Taŋka Pike Island

Minneapolis-
St. Paul
International
Airport

Mendota
Bridge

Mendota

Mni Sota Wakpa Minnesota River

● **Oheyawahe**
Pilot Knob

Mendota
Heights

0   1 mile

0   5 miles

USING DAKOTA PLACE-NAMES helps readers to remember the deepest history of this place, but the names given here are not the only correct ones. For example, the Mississippi was known as both Ħaħa Wakpa (river of the falls) and Wakpa Taŋka (great river). The word "bdote" means "where two waters come together," and it is applied to many places, but the confluence of the two great rivers was the most widely known Bdote.

Missionaries who worked to create written Dakota heard the soft *b* of the language as an *m*, and Dakota linguists have corrected the spelling. The earlier spelling is preserved, however, in the legal names of several Dakota communities. And finally, spellings can be corrected: Oheyawahi is now more accurately spelled Oheyawahe. ☾

Mni Sota Wakpa (Minnesota River) at Wita Taŋka (Pike Island).

was present in the magnificent Owamni-yomni, "whirlpool." Wanaġi Wita (Spirit Island), which used to exist below the falls, was part of this sacred area and known as a place where eagles gathered. The Dakota harvested tree sap and made maple sugar on Wita Waśte ("good island," Nicollet Island) just above the falls, and women went there to give birth. Mniħaħa (Minnehaha Falls), the beautiful waterfall flowing into Ħaħa Wakpa downstream from Owamniyomni, is a place of spiritual power and sacred water, which Dakota people visited to live, work, and play. Just upstream from the confluence, at Mni Sni (Coldwater Spring), water comes out of the earth, and Dakota people used it for medicine and ceremonies. The spring was also a meeting ground for Indigenous people of different nations. Mni Sni is at the base of Taku Wakaŋ Tipi ("something powerful dwells here," Morgan's Mound), which is the home of another Uŋkteħi. An underground river flows below the spring, out to Mni Sota Wakpa and into the world. For centuries, Mni Sni has been a place of healing, ceremony, and gathering.[3]

Wita Taŋka ("big island," Pike Island) and Oheyawahe (Pilot Knob) are located at the confluence. The Dakota named Oheyawahe "the place much visited" centuries ago; in the twenty-first century, Dakota elders gave it a second name, Wotakuye Paha, "the hill of the relatives." A Dakota tradition tells how the hill was formed. While chasing another creature,

Owamniyomni, later named
St. Anthony Falls. Engraving
by Seth Eastman, 1854.

Oheyawahe, later named
Pilot Knob. Watercolor
by Seth Eastman, 1846–48.

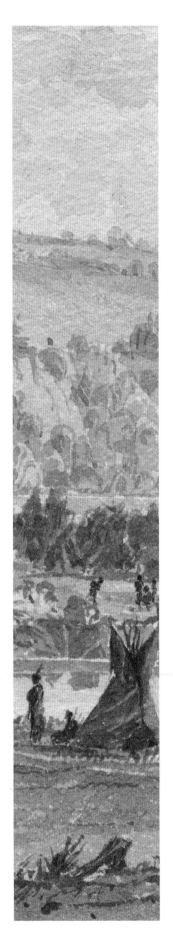

Uŋkteȟi plowed into the riverbank and raised up the hill. High above Bdote Mni Sota, the Dakota, Ojibwe, and Báxoje (Iowa) people came together on the great hill. Oheyawahe was a Dakota burial place for centuries and the setting for the Wakaŋ Wacipi—a health-giving medicine ceremony. Many Dakota wrapped up the bodies of their dead relatives and placed them on raised scaffolds before burying the bones in bundles.[4]

Further downstream, past the confluence, are the great burial mounds (now Indian Mounds Park) above Imniža Ska ("white cliffs," on St. Paul's east side)—and below them, Wakaŋ Tipi ("dwelling of the Great Spirit," Carver's Cave). Six caves associated with Uŋkteȟi used to exist at the site of Wakaŋ Tipi. For generations, Dakota people left pictographs inside the caves and held meetings before the entrances. Like their ancestors, the Dakota buried their dead in numerous great burial mounds across Mni Sota Makoce, and some brought their dead from afar for burial above Wakaŋ Tipi.[5]

These places are still here in Mni Sota Makoce, and they are still places of power.

People on the Land

Archaeologists, following the traditions of western science, have used excavations and radiocarbon dating to read evidence and establish theories about the past. They can show that people have lived in the land now called Minnesota for at least twelve thousand years, and they have named these people for types of pottery, projectile points, and mounds: Oneota, Hopewellian, Mississippian, and Psinomani. These are not the names the earlier residents would have called themselves—and the Dakota, along with other Indigenous peoples, claim the ancient inhabitants of Mni Sota Makoce as their ancestors. In the past, many archaeologists argued that scientific findings and traditional Indigenous knowledge were separate spheres of understanding. Archaeological knowledge was given prominence in their interpretations, which often had the effect of disconnecting the Dakota and other Indigenous people from their ancestors. Archaeologists recognize that they have only theories about where the Dakota people may have come from, and many scholars now acknowledge the importance of Dakota traditions, as Indigenous oral histories around the globe are proven to be accurate. Thus, the spheres of archaeology and Indigenous oral tradition are being combined, creating a place for shared authority and a more complex study of the past.

Archaeology tells us that when the glaciers receded about 12,500 years ago, the first humans appeared in what is now Minnesota. Glacial River Warren, which drained an immense lake covering what is now the Red River Valley, carved out the Minnesota River Valley and, along with other glacial waters, shaped Bdote. At the confluence of the Minnesota and Mississippi rivers, the earliest evidence of human life dates conservatively from eight thousand years ago, though human habitation likely dates to ten thousand years ago.[6]

By 8000 BCE (Before the Common Era) the river confluence hosted the intersection of pine and deciduous forests. Temperatures were cool, but rapidly warming. Animals such as deer, moose, wolves, coyotes, and bears likely inhabited the forests. The environment determined how people lived.[7]

People in the area around Bdote lived in small groups in a sparsely populated landscape. They were mobile hunters and foragers, traveling to gather different foods and resources in different seasons. Game animals were likely their main food source, augmented with fish

A projectile point, just over 5 inches long by 1 inch at maximum width, found at the site of the Henry H. Sibley House, located in Mendota. Archaeologists believe it is eight to twelve thousand years old.

Wita Taŋka (Pike Island).

and plants. Skilled craftsmen created projectile points and tools out of stone and wood. The oldest artifact found at Bdote is a projectile point made of stone dating from 10,000 to 8000 BCE. The oldest artifact found on the actual site of Historic Fort Snelling is another projectile point dating from 8000 to 6000 BCE. The lives of these Indigenous people probably focused on subsistence in this early period, but trade networks connected them to the rest of the continent. In an ancient grave dating from this period, people buried a member of their group with a pendant made of conch shell from the coast of present-day Florida.[8]

Dramatic changes in the environment began around 8000 BCE. As the climate became warmer and drier, tallgrass prairie entered what is now Minnesota from the southwest. By 6800 BCE it reached Bdote and passed further to the east. Some trees remained in large river valleys, like those of the Minnesota and Mississippi. The glacial lakes to the north melted more quickly and found other outlets, and the flow of Glacial River Warren ebbed. The dominance of the prairie at the river confluence lasted until roughly 4000 BCE, when cooler temperatures promoted the growth of oak forest.[9]

The archaeological record for this period (7500–3000 BCE) is sparse, but it is clear that the people in the region of Bdote continued to move often, hunting game and gathering plants throughout the area. Projectile points became smaller and were likely used with spear-throwers, called atlatls. The people hunted bison and woodland animals as the prairie covered the region and then retreated.[10]

Between 3000 and 500 BCE, the climate stabilized and vegetation zones mostly reached the position they occupied into the 1600s.

A leaf-shaped projectile point, 1.57 inches long and 1.54 inches at the base, found in 1973–74 by archaeologists digging under the portion of the original Fort Snelling hospital building that did not have a basement. Archaeologists estimate that it was used about 6000 BCE.

Craftsmen began using native copper to create adzes, awls, harpoons, and other tools. Some groups started burying their dead in communal burial sites. People began growing crops and harvesting wild rice, and the population increased. People in the Bdote region developed pottery between 1000 BCE and 500 BCE.[11]

Effigy and burial mounds, used for centuries, are the most lasting marks left by the people of this era. Around 200 BCE, people began burying their dead in mounds around Bdote. Builders often constructed mounds on high banks overlooking rivers and lakes. The most prominent concentration of mounds within the Bdote region, once numbering more than fifty, exists on the bluff overlooking the Mississippi at present-day Indian Mounds Park in St. Paul. Another sacred burial site sits on the northern side of the Minnesota River, in what is now Bloomington. Burial mounds were also built south of the river confluence, at present-day Mendota. To the west, up the Minnesota River from Bdote, burial mounds lined the riverbank.

The practice of mound building may have traveled up the Mississippi River from Cahokia, an American Indian cultural center that existed near present-day East St. Louis, Illinois. A community at what is now Red Wing, Minnesota, was a hub for the mound-building tradition, and its influence spread north to the confluence of the Minnesota and Mississippi

rivers and beyond until roughly 1000 CE (Common Era). New forms of pottery came with the burial mound tradition. In addition, people began constructing effigy mounds in the shapes of animals, humans, and symbols. These stylized mounds may have been used for spiritual purposes, and some were built near the great burial mounds at Imniża Ska. Migrants and trade linked the economy in Minnesota with the population center in the south.[12]

Society in the region of Bdote changed suddenly around 900 to 1100 CE. As corn became a major food source, larger bands of people began to live together, and archaeologists theorize they formed the first native tribes. Communities grew and became more permanent, and the area they controlled shrank. Some archaeologists hypothesize that the ancestral Dakota emerged in this period, near Bde Wakaŋ (Lake Mille Lacs), roughly around 1300 CE—a theory that aligns with one Dakota origin story. Another story places the origin of the Dakota far to the north, near the Arctic Ocean. One Dakota oral tradition says the Dakota immigrated to Mni Sota Makoce from the southeast part of North America; linguistic analysis supports this possibility. Regardless of where the Oyate came from, Mni Sota Makoce is Dakota homeland, and the Dakota connection to the land goes back beyond human memory.[13]

The Dakota Way of Life

"The ultimate aim of Dakota life, stripped of accessories, was quite simple," wrote Ella Deloria, a Dakota anthropologist of the early twentieth century. "One must obey kinship rules; one must be a good relative." This identity was absolute. "Every other consideration was secondary—property, personal ambition, glory, good times, life itself. Without that

aim and the constant struggle to attain it, the people would no longer be Dakotas in truth." The Dakota phrase "Mitakuye owasin"—"We are all related"—extended to visitors from far away, to animals and plants, and to the land itself.[14]

The Dakota existed within the bounty of that land, in relationship with all that is, and

Ice fishing in winter (detail). Watercolor by Seth Eastman, ca. 1846–48.

they lived according to the rhythms of the seasons. They lived throughout Mni Sota Makoce, from the northern woods to the southern plains. Their largest communities, summer planting villages, were located on lakes and rivers. The network of waterways near Bdote held several villages: along Mni Sota Wakpa and Ḣaḣa Wakpa from what is now Wabasha, upstream to Owamniyomni, up the Wakpa Wakaŋ (Rum River) to Bde Wakaŋ, along the Hoġaŋ Waŋke Kiŋ (St. Croix River), and along Mni Sota Wakpa west to the present Minnesota–South Dakota border. The Dakota traveled these rivers to trade and gather at Bdote for ceremonies. The only known Dakota village that may have been located directly at the confluence was Titaŋka Taŋnina or "the old village." Some traditions say this village was hundreds of years old, and groups of Dakota split off from it to establish other villages around Bdote. At some point Titaŋka Taŋnina moved south, across from where Bloomington is today. Just to the east was the village Ohaŋska (or Hohaanskae). Downstream from

the current site of St. Paul, near Imniża Ska on Ḣaḣa Wakpa, was Kap'oża. These summer villages were Bdewakaŋtuŋwaŋ, and the closest Dakota communities to the confluence itself.[15]

Dakota families made different choices about how and where to live, but most followed the annual movements of their communities. Bdoketu (summer) villages, made of semipermanent wooden lodges, were used for at least several years. Dakota women cultivated plots of corn, and they gathered and preserved berries, nuts, wild turnips, and other foods and medicinal plants while men hunted. In late summer, after harvesting corn, Dakota families packed up their belongings and moved to wild rice harvesting camps. Corn and rice were stored in underground pits for future use. Harvest was a time of abundance and ceremony for the Dakota people.

In Ptaŋyetu (fall), large groups dispersed to hunt deer. As game was depleted in one area, the group moved to another camp. Men did the hunting, while women moved supplies from camp to camp. Loads were kept light as

A Dakota summer planting community on Ḣaḣa Wakpa near the confluence. Watercolor by Seth Eastman, 1846–48.

more and more meat was gathered for wintertime. Hunters who were successful shared their meat, so that all would eat.

During Waniyetu (winter), smaller family groups made camp in wooded areas near summer village sites. Men hunted, fished, and trapped, while women maintained the encampments, dressed skins, and made clothing. Food stored during the summer harvest sustained the Dakota people through the harsh winters of Mni Sota Makoce.

As the air warmed in Wetu (spring), Dakota winter camps broke up and the people moved to maple sugaring camps. These sites usually had a semipermanent bark sugarhouse. Dakota women and children did most of the sugaring work, while men continued to hunt and trap. The Dakota brought their maple sugar harvest to the summer planting village sites, where the people gathered in their largest numbers and began the seasonal cycle again.[16]

The Arrival of the French

To the east of Bdote, French missionaries and traders began entering the Great Lakes region. The first European American record of the Dakota comes from Jesuit missionaries stationed among the Ojibwe in 1642. The Ojibwe told the Jesuits stories of a powerful people they called the "Nadouessis" living in large villages eighteen days to the west. The

"Nadouessis" harvested "Indian corn and Tobacco," noted the Jesuits. "Their villages are larger, and in a better state of defense, owing to their continual wars with the Kiristinons [Cree], the Irinions [Illinois] and other great Nations who inhabit the same Country." "Nadouessis" was the Jesuits' translation of the Ojibwe term "Nadowe Su." Some claim that the phrase means "people of an alien tribe," while others argue it is an insulting reference to snakes: "snake-like ones," or "lesser adders." It is thought the Ojibwe called the people to the west "Nadowe Su" because at times they were dangerous enemies. The French eventually translated "Nadowe Su" as "Su," which finally became "Sioux." By the nineteenth century, the Ojibwe used "bwaan" to mean Dakota.[17]

By the 1650s, before they ever saw a European, Dakota people had acquired European trade goods from Huron and Odawa refugees whom they had allowed to live for a time on an island in Ḣaḣa Wakpa south of Bdote (possibly Prairie Island). Trade goods, such as iron kettles, may have made it into the hands of Dakota people living near Bdote. Nicolas Perrot, a French fur trader and diplomat, described these events and the homeland of the Dakota as he saw them in the 1660s. Perrot wrote that the Dakota inhabited a region from Lake Mille Lacs south to the Minnesota River.[18]

The first recorded contact between the Dakota and French traders occurred in 1659–60. Pierre Radisson and Médard Chouart, Sieur des Groseilliers were wintering with an Ojibwe group in what is now Wisconsin when Dakota visited, bringing corn and wild rice to trade. Radisson said that he visited a Dakota village the next summer; while it is possible that he was in present-day Minnesota, it cannot be confirmed. Nicolas Perrot and the Dakota started trading on the upper portion of Ḣaḣa Wakpa in 1665. The Dakota were eager to obtain trade goods, especially weapons, as the Ojibwe had acquired firearms and begun moving into Mni Sota Makoce.[19]

Perrot or another French trader may have spent time at Bdote, but the first known European the Dakota welcomed there was Father Louis Hennepin. A Recollect friar, Hennepin was part of an expedition led by René-Robert Cavelier, Sieur de la Salle to explore the northern Mississippi. In March 1680, at Lake Pepin, the Frenchmen encountered a group of Dakota that escorted Hennepin and his companions to villages near Lake Mille Lacs. On the way to Mille Lacs, the travelers came to Owamniyomni. Hennepin recorded, "I named it the Falls of St. Anthony of Padua in gratitude for favors God did me through the intercession of that great saint, whom we chose as patron and protector of all our enterprises. The waterfall is forty or fifty feet high and has a small rocky island, shaped like a pyramid, in the center."[20]

Hennepin claimed the Dakota captured him, but the friar's account suggests they were interested in European technology and treated him as an honored guest. The Dakota allowed the three men to live with them until July of the next year, when a French military officer and explorer, Daniel Greysolon, Sieur du Lhut, found them, and they decided to return east with him.[21]

Before Hennepin left Mille Lacs, a Dakota leader drew him a map showing the way back to the French colony four hundred leagues away at Michilimackinac. Along the route, Hennepin and his companions came to Owamniyomni once again. Hennepin recorded a scene demonstrating how the Dakota people regarded the falls as sacred (as well as offering a European response): "While portaging our canoe at the Falls of St. Anthony of Padua, we caught sight of five or six of our Indians who had set out before us. One of them had climbed an oak across from the large waterfall and was weeping bitterly. He had a beaver robe dressed neatly, whitened inside, and decorated with porcupine quills, and was offering it in sacrifice to this cataract, which is terrifying and admirable." While at the falls, two of the

Frenchmen "took a beaver robe which Indians had attached to the trees in sacrifice." The Frenchmen passed through Bdote, continued south along Ḣaḣa Wakpa, and eventually returned east.[22]

La Salle journeyed down Ḣaḣa Wakpa in 1682, but he didn't mention the Dakota in his account. When he reached the mouth of the great river, the explorer invoked the Doctrine of Discovery and claimed the entire river and its watershed for the king of France. La Salle specifically listed the source of the river, beyond the homeland of the Dakota, as part of the new French "possessions." Although he had not visited the Dakota, he said they had consented to French control of their land. This nominal statement of land ownership was the first time a European power claimed the Dakota homeland.[23]

Nicolas Perrot returned to the homeland of the Dakota in 1688, and the next year he established Fort St. Antoine on Lake Pepin. He held a ceremony at the post to exercise the Doctrine of Discovery, much as La Salle had. Perrot claimed any place a Frenchman had visited to be part of the French empire, including Hoġaŋ Waŋke Kiŋ (St. Croix River), Bde Wakaŋ (Lake Mille Lacs), Bdote, and the mouth of Mni Sota Wakpa. Another Frenchman, Pierre Le Sueur, began trading among the Dakota in the region of Bdote in the 1680s. Le Sueur was probably among the first Europeans to pass through Bdote and ascend Mni Sota Wakpa. He and a trading party gave the name "St. Pierre" or "St. Peter's" to Mni Sota Wakpa sometime between 1683 and 1689, perhaps because they encountered it on St. Peter's Day—and because several members of their party were named Pierre. By 1700 Le Sueur was attempting to establish a trading post near present-day Mankato, but a group of Bdewakaŋtuŋwaŋ advised him that the confluence was a better place because it could serve them as well as the Báxoje and Otoes who lived to the south.

This advice given by the Dakota indicates that by 1700 the Báxoje and Otoe still lived in Mni Sota Makoce and visited Bdote. However, relations between the Dakota and Báxoje turned violent sometime in the 1700s as more Dakota obtained firearms. Writing in the late 1800s, missionaries recorded the Dakota tradition that the Báxoje had lived very close to the confluence and the last great battle between the Bdewakaŋtuŋwaŋ and Báxoje occurred on Oheyawahe, after which the Báxoje moved south. Like the Báxoje, the Otoe went south to avoid conflict with other Indigenous people who had obtained firearms from the French.[24]

An unknown Frenchman recorded the significance of Bdote to Dakota people on paper for the first time in about 1720. He noted that the Dakota believed the first Dakota man and

The Doctrine of Discovery

EUROPEAN MONARCHIES used the Doctrine of Discovery to legitimize the colonization of Indigenous lands and prevent the expansion of other European powers in the Americas. The claim—that Europeans could seize any lands not subject to a European Christian monarch—was the basis for European colonization from the 1500s to the 1900s. Invoking the doctrine involved ritualized ceremonies like those held by La Salle and Perrot. The listing of lands claimed, the shooting of muskets, and the invocation of king and country were necessary parts of the ceremony. The event included the manufactured consent of native peoples and frequently the planting of a cross or marker. Formal claims of land possession allowed European powers to transfer supposed land ownership through treaties and wars. In reality, most of these ceremonies had little practical effect, as Indigenous people kept their land and maintained their sovereignty. Like the French, the British and the United States used their own versions of the Doctrine of Discovery.[2] ☾

A leather coat modeled after a European frock coat and decorated with quillwork, possibly Cree, Métis, or Ojibwe in origin. It belonged to Alexander Ramsey and may have been brought back by him from an 1851 treaty signing.

woman came out of the ground on a prairie below Owamniyomni. In 1727 the French built the "Sioux Post" on Lake Pepin to trade with the Dakota under an official charter, and Dakota delegations visited Quebec and Montreal in the 1730s and '40s as the fur trade assumed more importance in their lives.[25]

The Dakota system of kinship and reciprocity was integral to the fur trade. Family bonds created trust and required people to share resources. Individuals did not need to be related by blood to be kin. French traders married into Dakota families, calling these unions *a la facon du pays*, or "according to the custom of the country"—essentially, Native marriage ceremonies adapted to the fur trade. Native women, who were always central to Indigenous society and governance, became pivotal figures in the trade. Their acceptance of European husbands extended kinship networks and created political and economic ties, as well. Without Native women, the structures

that governed the fur trade would not have functioned.[26]

As families blended, so did the material culture of Europeans and Dakota. Dakota people began using iron cookware and implements; firearms were highly valued. The Dakota incorporated the fur trade business into their seasonal cycles—trapping in the winter, when pelts were thickest and most valuable, and selling furs in the spring. European traders adopted Dakota foods and goods, such as clothing and canoes, and learned how to access Mni Sota Makoce's resources from their Dakota relatives. European-Dakota marriages created families of mixed ancestry, forming the basis of a borderland culture that existed for nearly two hundred years. Governed by native kinship networks, the diverse fur trade culture influenced politics and economics at Bdote and beyond until the 1860s.[27]

The fur trade era was a time of economic interaction and cultural blending, but it was also destructive to Indigenous culture, and it began European colonization of Mni Sota Makoce. At the state level, the French were practicing extractive colonialism. The government was interested in extracting furs from the region and used native people to access the land's resources. French occupation of the region was not always permanent and the land itself was not a key resource. But French incursions into native land paved the way for other colonists.[28]

As the fur trade became more entrenched, it destabilized relations between Indigenous peoples. The Ojibwe, growing in population, fleeing eastern conflicts, and following a prophecy that they would travel to where food

Drawing of a fur trader, 1830s, from the journal of Alexis Bailly, who ran the fur post at Mendota from 1823 until he was replaced by Henry Sibley in 1834.

grows on the water (wild rice), began moving into Mni Sota Makoce with permission from the Dakota. The Dakota and Ojibwe were more often allies than enemies, and sometimes they became family. The Dakota valued the Ojibwe as middlemen in the fur trade, but when the Dakota gained direct access to French traders, they became less willing to tolerate the Ojibwe incursions. Although trading, alliances, and familial ties continued, a series of sporadic, complex, and sometimes violent conflicts between the Dakota and Ojibwe began in 1736 and lasted more than a century. Drawn by the buffalo and new trading posts, the Dakota had already begun moving south, but the violence hastened their departure from the northern portion of Mni Sota Makoce.[29]

The British Take Over the Fur Trade

For nearly a century, the French claimed possession of Bdote through the Doctrine of Discovery. That changed after 1754, at the beginning of the Seven Years' War, an imperial contest spanning five continents and involving several European nations. In Britain's North American colonies, people called the conflict the French and Indian War, and it pitted the colonies of France and Britain against one another. Honoring ties of kinship and trade, the Ojibwe allied with the French during the war. The French were defeated in 1760 and forced to cede their North American possessions to Great Britain in 1763. The Dakota, now players in an imperial world, sent envoys to Montreal, where they described the Oceti Šakowiŋ to the British and asked that traders be sent to their land.[30]

In 1766 the British government sent explorer Jonathan Carver to the headwaters of Ḣaḣa Wakpa. At Lake Pepin he met a group of Dakota who allowed him to enter Bdote. Carver saw Wakaŋ Tipi, the cave that would be renamed for him, though the sacred site was only accessible by a narrow passage. Within was an underground lake in which the Dakota believed an Uŋktehi dwelt. On the walls were moss-covered petroglyphs. Carver noted a burial place of the Dakota nearby, which was likely the great mounds above the cave. The explorer moved upstream and ascended a height—Oheyawahe—that provided a view of Wita Taŋka and the mouth of Mni Sota Wakpa. At Bdote, Carver met a Ho-Chunk man and traveled with him up Ḣaḣa Wakpa to Owamniyomni, where, said Carver, the Ho-Chunk man threw his pipe, tobacco, and jewelry into the water and asked for its protection.[31]

After wintering with the Dakota on Mni Sota Wakpa, in April of 1767, Carver returned to Wakaŋ Tipi with a large group of Dakota who were bringing the remains of their relatives to Bdote for burial. When they reached Bdote, they conducted ceremonies and placed the remains in the mounds next to Wakaŋ Tipi. The Dakota held a "grand council" at the cave and allowed Carver to attend. According to Carver's account, it seems representatives of several Dakota communities were present to "settle their operations for the ensuing year." Carver stated that he was adopted as a Dakota chief, but more likely the Dakota adopted him as kin to cement their ties with Britain. The Dakota committed to peace with the English and again asked that traders be sent to them.[32]

British traders followed in Carver's wake and brought dramatic changes to the fur trade. Unlike the French, the British did not operate under government monopolies. In 1767 the fur trade was opened to any businessman who could raise the money to begin trading. For the British, capitalism, not kinship, guided the trade. While French traders had advanced goods against furs, they frequently forgave debt to preserve kinship ties and military alliances. The British made the credit system a purely economic one, rarely forgiving debt. Some traders purposefully kept their Dakota and Ojibwe customers in a state of indebtedness by marking up the price of goods. Anglo traders didn't interact with Indigenous culture as much as the French, but generations of European-Native people continued to be central to the trade.

For the rest of the eighteenth century, the fur trade between the Dakota and the British stabilized. However, the United States won its independence from Great Britain in 1783, and with the signing of Jay's Treaty in 1794, the British lost control of the Northwest. British and French traders formed their own companies or joined companies from the United States.[33]

Enter the United States

With the Louisiana Purchase in 1803, the United States claimed the western portion of the Mississippi River drainage, including the homeland of the Dakota—and Bdote. In 1805 an expedition led by US Army Lieutenant Zebulon Pike departed St. Louis, intent on exploring the headwaters of the Mississippi River. Unlike famous explorers Lewis and Clark, Pike did not set out under the US government's authority. Instead, the commander of the Missouri Territory, General James Wilkinson, who would be exposed after his death as a paid Spanish agent, ordered Pike's exploration. Pike's expedition was unique in its militaristic and colonial aims. The French and British had constructed posts in Mni Sota Makoce, but they were meant for trade, not military occupation. Wilkinson ordered Pike to find commanding spots to establish military posts and to obtain permission for their construction from the local Indigenous people.

Pike entered the Dakota homeland from the south by way of the Mississippi River. The first Dakota to meet him were Wabasha's people at the mouth of the Iowa River. Wabasha (The Leaf, also known as La Feuille) hosted Pike in his lodge and presented the lieutenant with a pipe to ensure he would "be treated with friendship and respect" as he met other Dakota on his journey north. Pike gave Wabasha gifts before departing and told the Dakota leader that the United States intended to establish posts in Mni Sota Makoce to trade with the Dakota.[34]

Afterward, the people who lived at Ḣe Mni Caŋ (Barn Bluff at Red Wing, also called Caske

Taŋka) welcomed Pike. Their leader Tataŋka-mani (Walking Buffalo, also called Red Wing) presented Pike with another pipe and accompanied him to Bdote, which they reached on September 21, 1805. Pike noted Dakota villages near Wakaŋ Tipi and Wita Taŋka, and he observed the Dakota bringing their dead to Bdote and placing them on scaffolds. Pike also encountered fur trader Jean Baptiste Faribault, encamped on the shore of the river. The US expedition made camp on the northeast point of Wita Taŋka, at the very center of Bdote.[35]

The next day, Cetaŋ Wakuwa Mani (Hawk that Hunts While Walking, also called Petit Corbeau or Little Crow; his grandson, also known as Little Crow, would be even more widely known to European Americans) arrived at Bdote with 150 men. The Bdewakaŋtuŋwaŋ

Lieutenant Zebulon Pike, about 1810.

Cetaŋ Wakuwa Mani or Little Crow, the leader of the Bdewakaŋtuŋwaŋ Dakota village of Kap'oża near Bdote in 1805. Lithograph by Charles Bird King, 1836.

climbed the bluff between Mni Sota Wakpa and Ḣaḣa Wakpa and saluted Pike by firing their weapons. Cetaŋ Wakuwa Mani and Pike agreed to a council the next day. On September 23, 1805, seven Dakota leaders met with Pike on the beach of Wita Taŋka under a bower made from the sails of Pike's vessel. Pike wrote, "I then addressed them in a speech, which, though long and touching on many points, had for its principal object the granting of land at this place, falls of St. Anthony, and St. Croix [river], and making peace with the Chipeways [Ojibwe]."

Pike drew up a document with three articles. The first granted the United States land for military posts at the mouth of the St. Croix River and at Bdote, up the Mississippi River to St. Anthony Falls. The United States would have "full sovereignty and power" over the land forever. The second article stated the United States would pay the Dakota for the land, but Pike left the amount blank. The final article promised the Dakota the right to travel across the land and use it as they always had. In his journal, Pike recounted, "It was somewhat difficult to get them to sign the grant, as they conceived their word of honor should be taken for the grant without any mark; but I convinced them it was not on their account, but my own, that I wished them to sign it." Of the seven Dakota leaders, only Cetaŋ Wakuwa Mani and Waŋyaga Inaźiŋ (He Sees Standing Up) signed the document.[36]

Dakota and US views about the land were very different. The United States saw the land as a commodity; the Dakota believed that the land could not be owned. Translating terms like "grant" and "sovereignty" would thus have been difficult. It is unlikely the Dakota leaders and US representatives understood the treaty provisions on the same terms.

There were several other problems with the agreement. The president of the United States had not authorized Pike's expedition, and therefore the army lieutenant had no legal authority to negotiate a treaty with any Indigenous people. Cetaŋ Wakuwa Mani and Waŋyaga Inaźiŋ's people lived near Bdote, but the two men did not have the power to represent thousands of Dakota. The Dakota people made important decisions through consensus, and most of their leaders were not present.

The US Senate did not discuss the agreement until 1808. The Senate unilaterally set the amount of land granted by the treaty at over fifty-one thousand acres at the St. Croix River and over one hundred thousand at Bdote, extending north up the Mississippi. Once the acreage was defined, the Senate set payment for the land at $2,000, though Pike had estimated its value at $200,000. No Dakota were present to agree to these terms. After the Senate ratified the treaty, President Thomas Jefferson did not proclaim it, which was standard procedure at the time. For these reasons, the "treaty" that set the legal groundwork for the construction of Fort Snelling was, in many ways, invalid. Even so, the US government continued to act as though it was a legally binding document.[37]

After Pike left Mni Sota Makoce, the Dakota continued trading with the British and had little or no contact with the United States. During the War of 1812, some Dakota supported the British and helped them regain territory in the Northwest, but the fledgling United States defeated the British in 1815, and the two nations agreed to reestablish their prewar borders. In 1815 and 1816 leaders of the Bdewakaŋtuŋwaŋ, Waḣpetuŋwaŋ, and Waḣpekute signed peace treaties stating that they were under the protection of the United States. The United States now claimed any land the Dakota people had ceded to other European powers, and any previous agreement made with the United States was confirmed.[38]

The United States Comes to Bdote

US Secretary of War John C. Calhoun drafted a plan in 1818 to build forts in the Upper Mississippi Valley that would extend US power westward, fulfill the government's economic and colonial ambitions, and ultimately play a pivotal role in taking control of Indigenous peoples' land. Calhoun wrote, "When these posts are all established and occupied . . . our northwestern frontier will be rendered much more secure than heretofore, and . . . the most valuable fur trade in the world will be thrown into our hands." It was not until 1818, thirteen years after the Dakota negotiated with Pike on Wita Taŋka, that the United States returned to Mni Sota Makoce. US Army Major Stephen Long traveled to Bdote, surveyed the place Pike had claimed, and reported that the confluence was the perfect location to construct a fort.[39]

In 1819 two arms of US colonialism converged on Bdote, one diplomatic and one military. In June Indian agent Major Thomas Forsyth began traveling up the Mississippi from St. Louis. His instructions were to distribute

Lieutenant Colonel Henry Leavenworth, about 1820.

approximately $2,000 in goods to Dakota leaders due to them under the terms of Pike's "treaty." That same summer, Lieutenant Colonel Henry Leavenworth, commanding the Fifth US Infantry Regiment in Detroit, was ordered to move the majority of his command to the confluence of the rivers. Leavenworth and ninety-eight men traveled across what is now Wisconsin and met Forsyth at Prairie du Chien. The two US government representatives set out for Bdote on August 8. Leavenworth, impressed with local trader Jean Baptiste Faribault's knowledge of the region, persuaded Faribault to accompany the expedition and establish a trading post at Bdote.

Forsyth arrived at Bdote on August 23, and Leavenworth, with his men, the next day. Forsyth made payments to Wabasha, Tataŋkamani, Cetaŋ Wakuwa Mani, Śakpe (The Six), and Penichon, among others. The military command established itself "on a place immediately at the mouth of [the] St. Peter's river, on its right bank." A few days later, Forsyth and Leavenworth visited Owamniyomni, which Forsyth described as "beautiful; the white sheet of water falling perpendicularly . . . over different precipices; in other parts, rolls of water, at different distances, falling like so many silver cords, while about the island large bodies of water were rushing through great blocks or rocks, tumbling every way, as if determined to make war against anything that dared to approach them."[40]

After completing his mission, Forsyth returned south. When 120 recruits joined Leavenworth's force in September, the total number of US soldiers at Bdote rose to just over two hundred. The command wintered in a wooden cantonment called New Hope, below the bluff, where the soldiers suffered from scurvy, dysentery, and cold. Over thirty of them died during the winter of 1819–20. Leavenworth moved his men to a new camp

A sketch of Cantonment New Hope made by Henry Rowe Schoolcraft in 1820. Pike Island is at left; cornfield and garden are in foreground; the long building at center left is the barracks, flanked by several other structures.

Indian agent Lawrence Taliaferro, about 1830.

near Mni Sni in the spring. The soldiers established Camp Coldwater at the ancient meeting ground. In the midst of the winter, as the men of the Fifth Infantry suffered, Calhoun reported to Congress that the post at the confluence would serve a vital purpose: "The post at the mouth of the St. Peter's is at the head of navigation on the Mississippi, and in addition to its commanding positions [*sic*] in relation to the Indians, it possesses great advantages, either to protect our trade, or prevent that of foreigners."[41]

The next summer Leavenworth asked the Dakota to meet with him in council to discuss the land agreement. The Dakota invited the Ojibwe as well: in the borderland between the two nations, they left a birch-bark pictograph depicting the US encampment at Mni Sni, along with Colonel Leavenworth and Śakpe, a Dakota leader. On August 1, 1820, an Ojibwe delegation met the Dakota at the sacred spring. Members of the two groups shook hands and smoked a pipe of peace together.

Josiah Snelling, about 1818.

One European American observer noted, "There was some indifference manifested to this treaty on the part of the Sioux" and some "could not be induced to smoke the pipe of peace, although the cessation of hostilities had their tacit consent."[42]

On August 9, 1820, Leavenworth and traders Duncan Campbell and Jean Baptiste Faribault met with twenty-two Dakota leaders from local bands at Mni Sni. Newly arrived Indian agent Lawrence Taliaferro, representing the president of the United States, was also present. The Dakota signed another agreement, this one granting land at the confluence of the rivers to the US government. The status of Native women was demonstrated when the negotiators granted Wita Taŋka to Pelagie Faribault, the French-Dakota wife of fur trader Jean Baptiste Faribault. The first Dakota to sign the document was Cetaŋ Wakuwa Mani. According to the agreement, the Dakota gave the land to the US government "in consideration of many acts of kindness received by said Indians from said Leavenworth." Payment for the land was alluded to, but not required. Locally, the treaty accomplished essentially the same goals as Pike's "treaty," but the US government never officially adopted the 1820 agreement.[43]

Shortly after the council at Mni Sni, Leavenworth was replaced by Colonel Josiah Snelling. Snelling was born in 1782 in Boston. He began a military career in 1803 as a sergeant in the Massachusetts militia, then joined the Fourth US Infantry Regiment in 1808 with the rank of first lieutenant. As a captain, he distinguished himself by leading a charge at the Battle of Tippecanoe in 1811. During the War of 1812 he was brevetted a major for bravery at the Battle of Brownstown. Snelling married Abigail Hunt in Detroit, and, after the war, he continued to rise in the ranks. On June 1, 1819, he was promoted to colonel of the Fifth Infantry Regiment and ordered to Bdote. Snelling oversaw the design of a diamond-shaped limestone fortification with the help of Lieutenant Robert

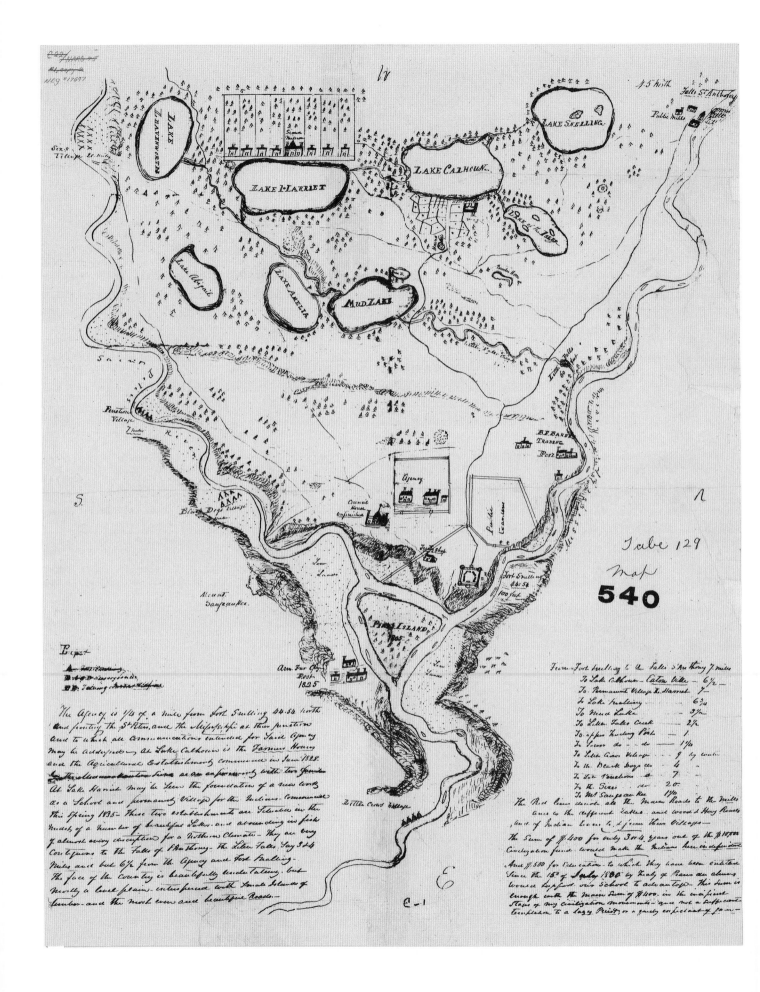

McCabe. Construction of Fort St. Anthony began on September 10, 1820.[44]

The US government's goals for the fort reflected its colonial aspirations. The post was intended to dissuade the British from any further incursions into the Northwest and to stamp out Anglo influence in the booming fur trade. The United States intended to exploit the region's resources for economic gain. Rather than protecting European American newcomers, the soldiers at Fort St. Anthony were tasked with keeping unauthorized people off Dakota and Ojibwe land so the fur trade could continue—until the land could be acquired through treaties. Finally, the United States sought to mediate the complex relationship between the sometimes clashing Dakota and Ojibwe. Peace between the two peoples would mean an uninterrupted flow of furs and tax revenue for the US government.

Bdote, which was important as a spiritual place and a meeting ground for Dakota people, was also the perfect strategic location for a nation with colonial aims. From the confluence of the rivers, the US military could control fur trade traffic in Mni Sota Makoce. The Dakota were far more powerful than the small garrison at Fort St. Anthony, but construction of the fort marked a seminal moment in the invasion of Dakota lands.[45]

Instead of building a wooden fortification typical of the time and region, Snelling opted for walls of stone. The fort was built of Platteville limestone quarried from the edge of the bluff. When completed, the structure was unlike anything in the Northwest. Batteries—towers housing artillery—secured each corner of the diamond. A hexagonal tower covered the approach from the landing on the river. On the western point of the fort, a round tower, complete with musket loopholes, faced out toward the prairie. To the north, a battery commanded traffic on the Mississippi River. The point of the limestone diamond facing the confluence of the rivers was capped with another battery that could control the river junction. The fort also included the commandant's house, two barracks for enlisted men, one for officers, and other essential buildings: schoolhouse, sutler store, commissary, guardhouse, powder magazine, and trade shops. Snelling remarked that the fort's "peculiar form was chosen to adapt it to the shape of the ground on which it stands." Fort St. Anthony was renamed Fort Snelling by General Winfield Scott in 1825, after he inspected the post.[46]

The fort was never directly attacked, and the most action soldiers experienced was tracking down fur traders who had broken government regulations. Routine, boredom, and hard labor were the lot of enlisted men in the post's early

Map of Bdote drawn by Indian agent Lawrence Taliaferro, 1835, showing the district and the multicultural community that existed there during the 1830s. At center is Wita Taŋka (Pike Island) and the confluence of the rivers. To the north of Wita Taŋka, Taliaferro drew his Indian Agency buildings at a larger scale than nearby Fort Snelling. To the south of Wita Taŋka, down H̄ah̄a Wakpa (Mississippi River), is the village of Kap'oża. To the southwest of Wita Taŋka is the community of Mendota, led by trader Henry Sibley. Up the Mni Sota Wakpa (Minnesota River) are the villages of Black Dog, Penichon, and Śakpe. Up the H̄ah̄a Wakpa is the trading post of B. F. Brook; this post and the associated buildings, where the Selkirk refugees lived, mark the location of Mni Sni (Coldwater Spring). At the far northwest corner of the map is Owamniyomni (St. Anthony Falls) and the public mills constructed there by the U.S. Army. At center-north is a Bdewakaŋtuŋwaŋ Dakota agricultural village at Bde Maka Ska (then renamed Lake Calhoun) led by Mah̄piya Wiçaśta. On the north shore of Lake Harriet (Bde Unma) is the Christian mission begun by Samuel and Gideon Pond in 1835.

years. Soldiers of the Fifth Infantry spent their first years at Bdote constructing the post as well as a mill at Owamniyomni. Isolated from US society, the garrison was sustained by a long supply chain that ran through the nearest town, St. Louis. Under Snelling's command the garrison began local food production. On the prairie outside the fort's walls, soldiers tended approximately four hundred acres of field crops and vegetable gardens. Blackbirds ruined the corn crop for many years. Soldiers performed various fatigue duties throughout the fort, and their lives were ruled by the schedule and discipline of the US Army.[47]

Married couples and their families lived in a barracks by the river until 1826, when a flood forced them to move into the fort. Their new quarters were probably in squad rooms and kitchens in the barracks. Wives of enlisted men were allowed to live at the post only if they worked as laundresses, hospital matrons, or domestic servants. Snelling and some subsequent post commanders were married, and their wives brought European American society to the fort. The commandant's house enhanced the commander's status as a gentleman and provided a space to entertain visitors according to social expectations. Several officers married Dakota women. Military strictures limited contact between enlisted men and the Dakota and Ojibwe. It is not known if enlisted men had consensual relationships with Dakota women, as did some of the officer class; while it is possible, the only known accounts appear to describe cases of sexual violence.[48]

The US government established the St. Peters Indian Agency on the fort's military reservation, and for the majority of its existence, from 1820 to 1839, it was administered by Lawrence Taliaferro. His main duties were to negotiate treaties, settle disputes between Indians and European Americans, enforce fur trade laws, and establish a good relationship with the Dakota and Ojibwe. Taliaferro also tried to

A Fifth Infantry Regiment bell crown shako, 1827, said to have been worn by a Captain Low. This style was nicknamed the tarbucket because of its shape and weight. *Courtesy Fort Winnebago Surgeon's Quarters Historic Site, photo by Paul M. Nelson.*

end violence between the Dakota and Ojibwe, which was destructive to the trade. However, Mni Sota Makoce was Indian country, and the United States had little real power.[49]

Motivated by expansionist goals, paternalism, and a belief that acculturation was the only way for Dakota and Ojibwe people to survive, Taliaferro and his successors encouraged Indigenous people to give up hunting and gathering and adopt European American agricultural methods. He also hoped to Christianize them, educate them according to European American standards, and end their traditional lifeways. After narrowly surviving a blizzard, Maȟpiya Wiçaṡta (Cloud Man), a Dakota leader from Ṡuŋka Sapa's (Black Dog's) band, decided to try the new ways. He and about two hundred men, women, and children made up the Dakota community that was established in 1829 under Taliaferro's oversight at Bde Maka Ska (Lake White Earth, renamed Lake Calhoun by colonists). Following Dakota tradition, they shared their crops with other Dakota—thus earning criticism from Taliaferro, who wanted them to be more self-interested, like European American farmers.[50]

In 1825 the US government called for a multinational gathering of American Indian tribes at Prairie du Chien, Wisconsin, which would codify peace and borders among the region's people: Dakota, Ojibwe, Ho-Chunk, Báxoje, Sauk, Meskwaki, and Menominee. Dakota and Ojibwe delegates gathered at Fort Snelling, and a party of 385 people traveled down Ḣaḣa Wakpa with Taliaferro. At the council, Indigenous leaders from several nations expressed dismay at defining the borders of their land, declaring that they held it in common, but in the spirit of peace they agreed. Bdote was solidly within acknowledged Dakota territory,

and it remained part of Dakota lands. For the first time, imaginary borders between Indigenous peoples were drawn through Mni Sota Makoce. Signing the treaty incorporated the Dakota, Ojibwe, and others in the region into the United States' colonial endeavors. With "legal" boundaries, the land was prepared for future acquisition by the United States. Five years later, the Waḣpetuŋwaŋ, Sisituŋwaŋ, Waḣpekute, and Bdewakaŋtuŋwaŋ returned to Prairie du Chien for another multinational gathering. In the ensuing treaty they ceded a strip of land between the Mississippi and Des Moines rivers, which when added to the lands ceded by the other nations, created a neutral ground. The treaty set aside a tract of land for people of European-Dakota ancestry along the Mississippi near Lake Pepin. For the first time the Dakota received annual payments, or annuities, of $2,000, for ten years. The US government also promised that a blacksmith would work for the Dakota and agricultural tools would be supplied to them.[51]

African Americans at Fort Snelling

The Northwest Ordinance of 1787 outlawed slavery in the Northwest Territory, which included Bdote, and the Missouri Compromise of 1820 banned slavery in the region. But it was common practice in the US Army for officers to have a personal servant or hold an enslaved person. Officers serving in southern regiments were accustomed to bringing their enslaved people with them around the country. US Army officers, government officials, and fur traders brought enslaved African Americans to Fort Snelling illegally. European Americans left no evidence of anyone protesting the existence of slavery there. Military, government, and business leaders at the confluence endorsed the practice by purchasing, owning, and selling enslaved individuals.[52]

Each army officer received extra pay to retain a servant, an expected practice in the US Army's rigid class structure. Some officers utilized enslaved labor instead, adding the extra pay to their overall income. Though the officer had to absorb the initial cost of purchasing or renting another human being, the extra pay mitigated this financial outlay and could boost the officer's income by 25 percent. Further, if an officer purchased a child, his initial cost was less, which encouraged the purchase of enslaved children. Officers submitted pay vouchers, often using the descriptor "slave," to collect this extra pay, which was provided to no other government officials. The US Army thus incentivized slavery and essentially paid its officers for being slavers. From 1819 to 1826,

Taliaferro listed the names of enslaved people he owned, with the annotation, "21 freed from slavery 1839–40–43," on the back of a document, dated July 13, 1813, that shows his membership in the Franklin Society.

Mary and Louisa were presumably cooks and performed domestic duties, while William was likely a personal attendant to Taliaferro and Snelling.[54]

The First US Infantry Regiment replaced the Fifth Infantry Regiment at Fort Snelling in 1828, and slavery at Bdote entered its peak years. The commander of the unit was Lieutenant Colonel Zachary Taylor, future president of the United States. Taylor brought two enslaved people with him named Jane and Glascon. He presided over an officer corps, made up mostly of southerners, that practiced slavery as a norm. Of thirty-eight officers at the post, thirty-three held an enslaved person at some point. At least seven enslaved people had lived at the fort under the Fifth Infantry, but under the First Infantry, the number swelled to thirty or more. Indian Agent Taliaferro seized the opportunity and imported more enslaved people to the confluence, becoming the region's largest slaveholder.[55]

The subagent at the Indian Agency, Elias T. Langham, played a prominent role in the practice of slavery at the fort. He frequently traveled to St. Louis, and officers often asked him to purchase enslaved people while there. In 1831 Taliaferro recorded a mysterious and painful event related to enslavement in Langham's household: "Mr. Langhams little Daughter—3 years & better old—was taken off—by some person unknown this morning struck several severe blows on the head—which rendered her senseless[.]" The next day Taliaferro wrote, "An Iron collar—Ball & chain & hand cuffs put on—Mariah their [sic] servant girl of Mr. Langham—who confessed to the fact of being the cause of the injury to his little daughter received but not with the intent to kill." The journal gives no further evidence, leaving unanswerable questions even as it provides a glimpse at Mariah's lived experience.[56]

As the number of enslaved people at the river confluence grew, slavery spread beyond Taliaferro and the military. Captain John

at least 10 percent of the Fifth Infantry's officers held enslaved people.

Indian agent Lawrence Taliaferro brought at least three enslaved people with him to Bdote. From time to time he rented his enslaved people out to army officers, including Colonel Snelling, who rented William, a man enslaved by Taliaferro. Snelling himself joined the ranks of slaveholders when he purchased a woman named Mary and her daughter Louisa at St. Louis in 1827. The colonel brought them to the fort and listed them as "slaves" on his pay claims.[53]

We know little about the enslaved people at Fort Snelling, but can make some informed suppositions about their daily lives. They most likely slept in the kitchens they worked in, or in doorways and hallways outside the rooms of the person they were attached to. The people Snelling enslaved probably stayed in the basement kitchen of his home. Enslaved people provided skilled manual labor at the fort.

Garland sold an enslaved woman named Courtney to fur trader Alexis Bailly in 1831. Courtney was either pregnant with or had already given birth to her son Joseph Godfrey, the only person known to have grown up as an enslaved person in what became Minnesota. In 1833 Bailly sold an enslaved woman to his father-in-law, Jean Baptiste Faribault. Chief among the traders at Mendota was Henry Hastings Sibley, who arrived in 1834 to run the American Fur Company operations in the region. Sibley, who would play a central role in the history of Minnesota, employed a "mulatto" cook named Joseph Robinson, who was probably owned by another trader.[57]

Records show that some military officers and civilians whipped and beat enslaved people at Bdote. In the mid-1840s the body of an enslaved woman was found just downriver from Fort Snelling. The woman had been enslaved by an army captain, but he claimed he could not recognize the body. After the case was closed, it came to light that the woman had been whipped to death and thrown into the river in the middle of the night. The army captain was never investigated. Bdote was hundreds of miles away from other US population centers, and enslaved African Americans had little hope of escape. Even if a runaway reached another community, there was no telling if local authorities would provide protection under the law. Joseph Godfrey, who grew up speaking Dakota and English, escaped slavery; he lived among the Dakota.[58]

The only enslaved African American at Fort Snelling known to have secured his freedom and live in Minnesota was James Thompson. Thompson was born into slavery in Virginia and brought to Fort Snelling by John Culbertson of St. Louis in 1827. The next year Lieutenant William Day, a New Yorker of the First Infantry, purchased Thompson; five years later Thompson, who was evidently learning the Dakota language, married a Dakota woman, a daughter of Maȟpiya Wiċaśta (Cloud Man). His ability with the language caught the attention of Alfred Brunson, a Methodist missionary who arrived at Bdote in 1837 and needed a translator. In May of 1837, with funds raised from friends in the East, Brunson paid for Thompson's freedom. Thompson worked as an interpreter for two years and lived near the Fort Snelling military reservation. In the 1840s Thompson and others founded a community called Pig's Eye, which eventually became St. Paul, where he did carpentry work and erected some of the town's first buildings.[59]

Enslaved African Americans and the Fight for Freedom

The vast majority of enslaved people at Fort Snelling had no legal recourse to defend themselves. Yet, four enslaved people—Courtney, a woman named Rachel, and the famous married couple Dred Scott and Harriet Robinson Scott—are known to have challenged their illegal enslavement at Fort Snelling in the courts.

Elias T. Langham procured Rachel at St. Louis in 1830 for Lieutenant Thomas Stockton. Stockton enslaved Rachel at Fort Snelling for a year and then at Fort Crawford at Prairie du Chien until 1834. While at Fort Crawford, Rachel gave birth to a son, James Henry. Stockton took Rachel and her son to St. Louis and sold them to a slave dealer. Rachel sued for her freedom in a Missouri court, arguing that she had been illegally enslaved in free territory at Fort Snelling and Prairie du Chien. In June 1836 the Missouri Supreme Court ruled in her favor, and Rachel and her son were set free.[60]

Courtney's case overlapped with Rachel's. Alexis Bailly sold Courtney and her son William to a prominent slaveholder in St. Louis in 1835. Courtney sued for her freedom and

Illustration of Dred and Harriet Robinson Scott from *Frank Leslie's Illustrated Newspaper,* June 27, 1857.

convinced a lawyer to take her case. With Rachel's case ongoing, Courtney deemed it prudent to wait for a decision. When Rachel was declared free, Courtney became free as well.[61]

Even though Rachel and Courtney's freedom suits affirmed that enslavement was illegal at the confluence, the practice continued. The number of enslaved people at Fort Snelling dropped off dramatically in 1837 when the First Infantry went south to fight in the US–Seminole Wars and the Fifth Infantry returned to the post. As before, the officers of the Fifth did not hold as many enslaved people as those of the First, but the captain in command, Martin Scott, did.[62]

At about this time, the makings of another lawsuit were brewing. Harriet Robinson was born into slavery, likely in Virginia around 1820. Lawrence Taliaferro either inherited

or purchased her and brought her to Bdote around 1835. In 1836 US Army surgeon Dr. John Emerson arrived at Fort Snelling and brought with him an enslaved man named Dred Scott. Like Harriet Robinson, Dred Scott had also been born into slavery in Virginia sometime around 1800. His owners, the Blow family, moved to St. Louis and sold him to Emerson, who was stationed at Jefferson Barracks. Over the next twelve years, Emerson brought Scott with him to military posts in Illinois and Wisconsin Territory—and eventually to Fort Snelling. Little is known about the early lives of Dred and Harriet, or how they met.

In 1836 or 1837 Dred and Harriet were married in a ceremony officiated by Taliaferro, the highest US civil authority in the area, at a time when marriages of enslaved people were not legally binding. Afterward, Taliaferro either gave or sold Harriet to Dr. Emerson. The newly

FORT SNELLING AT BDOTE

married couple lived within the walls of the fort, likely in the kitchen below Dr. Emerson's quarters at the east end of the post hospital. Sometimes officers rented the services of the Scotts while Emerson was away. At one point, the Scotts briefly served Emerson when he was posted to Fort Jesup, Louisiana, in 1838. Later in the year they accompanied Emerson back to Fort Snelling. On the return trip, while in free territory, Harriet gave birth to their first daughter, Elizabeth (Eliza).

In 1842 Emerson and the enslaved Scotts returned to St. Louis. Emerson died the next year, and his widow, Irene Sanford Emerson, took ownership of Dred, Harriet, and their daughter. The Scotts attempted to buy their freedom, but Emerson refused. Their second daughter, Lizzie, was born in 1846, and the Scotts feared the prospect of their family being separated. Aided by local abolitionists, and perhaps inspired by the freedom suits of Rachel and Courtney, the Scotts sued for their freedom in 1846 and 1847 in the Missouri courts. Their first case was thrown out on the technical grounds that no witnesses could prove they had been enslaved by Emerson at Fort Snelling or another northern post. The Blow family aided Dred and Harriet when they sued again in 1847. In January 1850 the Scotts were granted their freedom, but Irene Emerson appealed the case and it eventually made its way to the Missouri Supreme Court in 1852. The state supreme court went against the precedent of Rachel and Courtney's cases, ruling that the Scotts were to remain enslaved.

Irene Emerson married Dr. Calvin Chaffee in 1850. Chaffee, an abolitionist, was seemingly unaware of the Scotts' freedom suit. In 1853 Irene Sanford Emerson Chaffee's brother, John Sanford, who lived in New York, began claiming ownership of the Scotts. The Scotts then sued in federal court, because their enslavement involved owners in two states. They lost the case in 1853 but appealed the next year. The case *Scott v. Sandford* was heard by the US Supreme Court in 1856. In 1857 Chief Justice Roger B. Taney handed down the court's decision. The court ruled that African Americans were not citizens, and therefore the Scotts had no right even to sue. Further, the ruling overturned the Missouri Compromise and other acts concerning enslavement in the expanding nation. The court decided that slave owners could take their property anywhere in the United States—essentially declaring the entire country to be slave territory. The decision enflamed the country and helped lead to the American Civil War.[63]

By the time of the Dred Scott US Supreme Court case, Calvin Chaffee was a US congressman. He found out too late that his wife was the owner of the Scotts and was called a hypocrite in the press. After the decision, Chaffee transferred ownership of the Scotts to the Blow family. Taylor Blow signed the Scotts' manumission papers on May 26, 1857. The Scotts lived in St. Louis, where Harriet worked as a laundress and Dred found employment at a hotel. Dred died in 1858, and Harriet in 1876.[64]

As these freedom suits were pursued, slavery continued at Fort Snelling, ending just before Minnesota statehood in 1858, with only a brief hiatus from 1845 to 1850. The practice of slavery spread to Fort Ridgely in western Minnesota in 1854. From 1855 to 1857, no fewer than nine people were enslaved at Fort Snelling, the highest number since the 1830s. Slavery at the fort did not end because of legal action. The Tenth US Infantry, the last slaveholding unit to garrison the fort, was transferred to Utah in 1857.[65]

ancestry, frequently called métis ("mixed" in French). Some of the enslaved African Americans living at Bdote also became kin to the Dakota. The Selkirk refugees joined the community, bringing Swiss and Scottish people to the population.[69]

Though the Dakota had allowed the US Army, fur traders, and colonists to reside at Bdote, the district maintained its sacredness. Dakota people continued to visit the nearby places of power, to hold councils there, and to bury their dead at Imniża Ska above Wakaŋ Tipi and at Oheyawahe. Bdote continued to be an important place for diplomacy and trade, as it had been for centuries.

The Treaties of 1837

As the community at Fort Snelling and Bdote grew in the 1830s, it also began to splinter. Local and global forces led to the decline of the fur trade. In the eastern part of Mni Sota Makoce, fur-bearing animals and game had become less abundant, and silk replaced fur as the most fashionable material for hats in Europe. The decline of the trade sent ripples through the local economy. A Bdewakaŋtuŋwaŋ man told Indian Agent Taliaferro, "It seems everything is changed for the worse." Traders, government officials, missionaries, Dakota leaders, and Ojibwe leaders realized something needed to be done.

Traders like Sibley and Bailly looked for ways to diversify their business. As European Americans like the Selkirk refugees and other civilians slowly moved into the area, they became the traders' customers. Farmers and loggers began trickling into the region, and some squatted on native land. Sibley started managing the sutler store at Fort Snelling, obtained government supply contracts, and ran the local mail service. Traders had normally opposed treaties in the past, believing that US expansion would spell doom for the fur trade. However, the traders realized the end of the fur trade was near, and a treaty that required the Dakota and Ojibwe to pay the traders' claimed debts could provide financial salvation.

Local missionaries like the Pond brothers also supported a land cession by the Dakota.

They hoped a new treaty would provide money to support mission schools. St. Peters Indian Agent Taliaferro began pushing for a treaty in 1836. He, too, wished to acculturate the Dakota, but he genuinely hoped to serve their interests. Taliaferro despised the traders and thought a treaty would end their economic influence over the Dakota. He also felt the Dakota could be saved if they adopted European American agricultural methods.

In 1836 Mni Sota Makoce became part of what the US government called Wisconsin Territory, with the Missouri River as its western boundary. Henry Dodge, appointed the territory's governor and superintendent of Indian Affairs, wanted to remove American Indian people from the eastern portion of the territory as quickly as possible to fulfill the goals of the Indian Removal Act of 1830 and begin the US takeover of the region. Instead of attempting to stop the illegal logging of forests on Dakota and Ojibwe land, Dodge said the logging could not be stopped and, therefore, paying Indians for their land was the most ethical thing to do.[70]

At Bdote, the Dakota struggled to make a living off the land as its resources were depleted. They became outraged as lumbermen and farmers began illegally exploiting natural resources and moving onto Dakota and Ojibwe lands without permission. Many Dakota and Ojibwe people were entangled in the fur trade's credit system, which left them indebted and unable to obtain trade goods. Traders increasingly worked with only the people they deemed good financial risks; capitalism had replaced kinship as the operating principle. Dakota and Ojibwe leaders understood the power of cash, and they had witnessed the treatment of land as a commodity. Some of them began to feel a small cession of land could be an answer to their problems. Taliaferro, the main proponent of a treaty, eventually convinced the Dakota and Ojibwe to consider a land cession.

On July 20, 1837, over a thousand Ojibwe gathered at Fort Snelling to listen to Governor Dodge and negotiate a land deal. Lawrence Taliaferro, Captain Martin Scott (then in command of Fort Snelling), and Henry Sibley were also present. Serving as one of the interpreters was Stephen Bonga, one of the earliest people of African descent to live in Mni Sota Makoce. Bonga was the son of Pierre Bonga, an African American man, and a woman known as Ogibwayquay, which means Ojibwe Woman. Stephen Bonga and his well-known brother George worked in the fur trade for the American Fur Company. Both were important cultural intermediaries between the Ojibwe people, fur traders, and the US government.[71]

Negotiations took place over several days under an arbor erected outside the walls of the fort. Though relations were sometimes tense, the Dakota and Ojibwe did not engage in conflict with one another. From the start, Governor Dodge was aggressive, alternately pushing the Ojibwe to sell their land and promising to give them more time to decide. At first the Ojibwe leaders resisted, stating that their relatives who actually lived on the land in question had not yet arrived. After five days, more Ojibwe from what is now northwestern Wisconsin joined the negotiations. Stephen Bonga and the other interpreters presented the Ojibwe leaders with a map showing the United States' proposition. When a deal seemed close, the traders rushed to have their claims—real

or not—paid through the treaty. Taliaferro became so incensed by trader Lyman Warren, who brought hundreds of Pillager Ojibwe with him to press a claim, that he drew his pistol and threatened to shoot Warren. However, a faction of the Ojibwe wanted the traders paid, and eventually $70,000 was provided for that purpose. On July 29, 1837, the assembled Ojibwe leaders agreed to the land sale. The Ojibwe forced a rare provision into the treaty, despite the traders' scheming and pressure from Dodge. The Ojibwe retained the right to hunt, fish, gather wild rice, and otherwise use the land as they always had. The Ojibwe also made sure their relatives of mixed ancestry were provided with a $100,000 payment.[72]

After signing the treaty with the Ojibwe, the US government turned to the Dakota. Taliaferro, angered by the traders' role in the treaty with the Ojibwe, sought to avoid the same machinations against the Dakota. The Indian agent decided to have a treaty negotiated with the Dakota in Washington, DC, but the traders warned they would obstruct his plan unless he assured them their interests would be represented. Hoping to outwit the traders, Taliaferro secretly assembled Bdewakaŋtuŋwaŋ, Waȟpekute, Waȟpetuŋwaŋ, and Sisituŋwaŋ leaders, and the delegation traveled to Washington, DC. The Dakota leaders knew the value of the land in question and initially asked for $1.6 million. The US representatives rejected that amount. The Dakota, hoping to help their economically struggling people, did not want to go home empty-handed.

Maȟpiya Nażiŋhaŋ (Standing Cloud) said, "We never dreamt of selling you our lands until your agent our Father invited us to come and visit our Great Father. The land that we give up to you is the best that we have. We hope that you will allow us to hunt on it." Another leader named Ehake stated that the Dakota wanted "to reserve the islands in the river so that we can go and cut wood." On September 29, 1837, the Bdewakaŋtuŋwaŋ and Waȟpekute leaders

ceded all their land east of Ḣaḣa Wakpa, while the Waḣpetuŋwaŋ and Sisituŋwaŋ did not sign. The treaty also ceded the islands and did not include the Dakota's right to hunt on the ceded land. This cession technically included Wakaŋ Tipi and the ancient burials above the cave. In return, the Dakota signers received a trust from which they would be paid an annual annuity. Additionally, they were to be given $25,000 in goods annually for twenty years and a one-time payment of $10,000 for agricultural tools and livestock. Like the Ojibwe, the Dakota made sure their relatives of mixed ancestry received a substantial payment. Even though Taliaferro had tried hard to avoid the traders' influence, Henry Sibley, Alexis Bailly, and others followed the delegation to Washington and forced a provision into the treaty that provided $90,000 for the traders. The Dakota consented to the payment and signed the treaty on September 29, 1837.[73]

The Dakota and Ojibwe likely found the sale of their lands painful, but they believed the treaty had brought security to their people. Confident the traders would be paid off, and anticipating delivery of goods and annuities, many Dakota and Ojibwe decided not to participate in the fur trade that season. This choice led to disastrous consequences. The treaty was not ratified until June of 1838, and the first payment of money and goods did not arrive at Fort Snelling until October of 1839. The first shipment was disbursed to the Ojibwe near present-day Stillwater, but it was mostly made up of items such as fine cloths and handkerchiefs instead of firearms, tools,

and other useful things. The Ojibwe were unable to transport what food they did receive as the waterways froze up. The Dakota were informed they would not be paid their annuity until the following year, and many of them faced starvation. When they finally received their payments, their immediate needs were met, but most of the money went to the American Fur Company to satisfy their debts. In marked contrast, the traders did not experience a similar delay in their payments.

Loggers, speculators, and homesteaders arrived on the ceded land before the treaties were ratified. Squatters living on the Fort Snelling military reservation moved across the river and built cabins; the Dakota village of Kap'oża moved from the east side of Ḣaḣa Wakpa to the west side. The 1837 treaty also left the Dakota ancestral homeland around Bdote lawless. With the Fort Snelling garrison down to fifty men, and ineffective civil authority in the area (Taliaferro resigned in 1839 and was replaced with a less able agent), traders could operate without licenses, sell whiskey, cut down timber, build sawmills, and stake claims. One entrepreneur even earned money by forcibly removing Bdewakaŋtuŋwaŋ people to the west side of Ḣaḣa Wakpa. When annuities finally arrived, the Bdote fur trade morphed into what was known as the Indian trade. Traders continued to extend credit to the Dakota but preferred payment in hard cash instead of furs. Dakota people and other American Indians began paying for trade goods with annuity money.[74]

Territorial Transition

The US War Department moved to define the boundaries of the Fort Snelling military reservation in 1837 as land at Bdote became a real estate commodity. By this time, Major Joseph Plympton was in command of Fort

Snelling, and it fell to him to survey the reservation. Because Pike's agreement with the Bdewakaŋtuŋwaŋ and Leavenworth's unofficial treaty both lacked specifics, Plympton was able to redefine the boundaries of the military reservation. Plympton and his cohorts, motivated by a chance to control the natural resources at Bdote, extended the new reservation far beyond anything the military had previously claimed. On the west side of Haȟa Wakpa it included almost all the lakes in present-day Minneapolis and, more importantly, Owamniyomni and the mill there. The military claimed a wide swath of land on the east side of the river, which had just been ceded by the Bdewakaŋtuŋwaŋ and Waȟpekute. The new military reservation line jumped to the south side of Haȟa Wakpa and Mni Sota Wakpa, claiming more land than ever before. The land claim stretched up Mni Sota Wakpa and encompassed land on which the long-established Bdewakaŋtuŋwaŋ summer villages of Ohaŋska and Titaŋka Taŋnina lay.

The results of the survey threatened the livelihoods of the Selkirkers and itinerant traders living at Mni Sni and across the river at a hamlet known as Rumtown. Unlicensed traders living at Bdote also feared eviction. Beginning with Colonel Snelling, post commanders had normally allowed citizens to settle on the military reservation, but with the arrival of more US civilians, that practice ceased. By 1840 the US Army had removed all of the squatters on the military reservation and burned their homes. Many of the squatters moved to the area near Wakaŋ Tipi and Imniża Ska, where they founded the city of St. Paul.[75]

The Dakota remained at the center of the region's economy during the 1840s. The annuity money they spent became the main source of cash along the rivers. In 1842 the American Fur Company went bankrupt. Some traders shifted from furs to the Indian trade and marked up the cost of goods in an effort to force the Dakota back into debt. Other traders, disgusted with the exploitive practices, quit the business altogether. Profiteers did all they could to extract money from the Dakota. Continued European American immigration into

the area brought pressure for another treaty to be signed.

The concept of a permanent "Indian Territory" far to the west had been proposed since the 1820s. In 1840 the governor of Wisconsin Territory, James Doty, advocated for a new treaty that would make the idea a reality. The Doty Treaty proposed that the Dakota homeland west of Haȟa Wakpa would become a vast "Indian Territory" where the Dakota, Sauk, Meskwaki, and Ho-Chunk would live, permanently separated from European American society. Looking to have their claimed debts paid, Sibley and the traders supported this proposal. On July 31, 1841, leaders of the Sisituŋwaŋ, Waȟpetuŋwaŋ, and Waȟpekute, seeing the treaty as permanent protection of their ancestral lands, signed at Traverse des Sioux. Four days later, some Bdewakaŋtuŋwaŋ leaders signed the treaty at Bdote, while others refused to consider it. The treaty died in Congress, but it foreshadowed the land cessions to come.[76]

The kinship ties of the fur trade that had bound American Indians and newcomers together for nearly two hundred years were coming apart. As US society was planted at places like St. Paul, the racism of European Americans who had lived in the borderland culture came to the fore. Officers at the fort, and some traders, abandoned their marriages with Dakota women and distanced themselves from their mixed-race children. Lawrence Taliaferro left his Dakota wife, Aŋpetu Inajiŋwiŋ, in 1828 and married Eliza Dillon while on furlough back east. That same year, Aŋpetu Inajiŋwiŋ gave birth to Taliaferro's daughter, Mary. When Taliaferro left Fort Snelling forever in 1839, he left Mary behind with the missionary Samuel Pond. Henry Sibley left Ta Śina Duta Wiŋ in 1842, and she died the following year. Sibley watched over their daughter, Helen or Wahkiŋye, from afar, placing her in a missionary school. In 1843 Sibley married Sarah Jane Steele, who was the sister of local

come to Mni Sota Makoce in 1820 as a soldier in the Fifth Infantry and then traded at the confluence. Like Sibley, Brown had begun transitioning his business as more immigrants arrived. Sixty-one delegates, almost all of Anglo American ancestry, met to elect a representative to travel to Washington with a petition asking the federal government to create the new territory. Henry Sibley was elected, and his efforts culminated in the formation of Minnesota Territory on March 3, 1849. The new political entity was made up of the ancestral lands of the Dakota and Ojibwe. The opinions of more than thirty thousand Indigenous people were not considered in the matter.[79]

Newly appointed territorial governor Alexander Ramsey and the territorial legislature hoped to keep as many Dakota and Ojibwe people in the territory as possible because the local economy still depended on their annuities. But that attitude quickly shifted as US government officials turned their gaze toward Dakota lands west of the Mississippi River. Once again, Sibley and the traders claimed debts against the Dakota and were looking for a final treaty to recoup their money and extricate themselves from the trade once and for all. Ramsey, Sibley, and others agreed that the entirety of the land had to be taken from the Dakota while simultaneously keeping them within the territory so their annuity money could support the territorial economy.[80]

The Treaties of 1851

In 1851 Territorial Governor Alexander Ramsey, along with Henry Sibley, as territorial delegate to Washington, DC, gained permission to negotiate a treaty that would extinguish Dakota ownership of nearly all their ancestral lands and concentrate the people on a small reservation away from colonists. Unlike the Bdewakaŋtuŋwaŋ, the Waȟpetuŋwaŋ, Sisituŋwaŋ, and to a lesser extent the Waȟpekute did not receive substantial annuities from any previous treaties, and they were in more dire economic straits than their Bdewakaŋtuŋwaŋ kin. Ramsey and the other treaty commissioners devised a strategy to divide and conquer the Dakota. Following the advice of trader Martin McLeod, they planned to negotiate first with the Waȟpetuŋwaŋ and Sisituŋwaŋ, who would be more likely to sign a treaty. Seizure of their lands would then be used as leverage against the Bdewakaŋtuŋwaŋ and Waȟpekute, who would be surrounded by the United States and isolated from the rest of the Dakota.

On June 30, 1851, a party consisting of Ramsey, Sibley, Commissioner of Indian Affairs Luke Lea, and traders arrived at Traverse des Sioux to negotiate with the Dakota of the upper Mni Sota Wakpa. Ta Oyate Duta of Kap'oża accompanied the party. The treaty negotiation brought together many people in a culmination of fur trade society: Dakota men, women, and children; fur traders of French, English, and American descent; métis people; and US citizens, government officials, and soldiers all gathered. Ramsey and Lea pressured the Dakota to come to a decision quickly, and from the beginning the Dakota resisted, wishing to wait for more of their relatives to arrive. Dakota communities reached decisions by consensus, and the treaty commissioners deliberately tried to disrupt that process. Talks lasted several days, and at points the discussions nearly broke down. Henry Sibley, representing the traders, negotiated with the Dakota off the record.[81]

On July 23, the Dakota leaders reluctantly signed the Treaty of Traverse des Sioux. Like previous treaties, it provided annuities and funds for farming equipment and building materials—all meant to facilitate the Dakota's acculturation and pressure them to give

up their traditions and become like European Americans. The treaty confined the Dakota to a reservation on the upper reaches of Mni Sota Wakpa. Dakota leaders were then directed to sign another document, which came to be known as the "traders' paper." It authorized direct payments to the traders from the US government, completely bypassing the Dakota. The document was not explained, and many European American observers had never seen it before. Its provisions went against the wishes of the Dakota, who intended to pay the traders themselves. After concluding the treaty, Ramsey and the commissioners traveled down Mni Sota Wakpa to Bdote.[82]

The stage was set for one of the most consequential events that ever took place at the confluence. The Bdewakaŋtuŋwaŋ and some Waȟpekute had already begun to gather at Bdote when the US representatives arrived at Mendota on July 25, 1851. The treaty commissioners were intent on replicating the terms the western Dakota had agreed to. Negotiations started on July 29 in a warehouse at Mendota. Ramsey and Lea began by saying it was time for the Bdewakaŋtuŋwaŋ and Waȟpekute to give up their lands so immigrants would have room to live. Ramsey stated, "For at the same time, these lands have ceased to be of much value to you, from the rapid disappearance of the game, they have become more valuable to [the president's] white children." He then delivered the blow of Traverse des Sioux: "And besides, the question of sale has assumed a more interesting aspect to you, since your brothers, the Sissitons and Wahpetons, have disposed of their lands to the rear of you. So that hereafter you would not only have the whites along the river front, but all around you." Wabasha declared that the Dakota would not negotiate a new treaty because the US government owed them money from the 1837 agreement.[83]

The next day talks reconvened under an arbor on the north slope of Oheyawahe just above the riverboat landing at Mendota. The site provided a commanding view of Bdote and Fort Snelling. Ramsey, Lea, and the other commissioners sat at tables, surrounded by a semicircle of Dakota leaders. Wabasha stood and rejected the treaty outright. Wakute said, "Our habits are different from those of the whites, and when we have anything to consider it takes us a long time." Lea disregarded the Dakotas' protests, saying, "They are chiefs and men, not women and children; and they can certainly be prepared to give us an answer tomorrow."[84]

The next day, Ta Oyate Duta raised the issue of the 1837 money again. Lea used the 1837 money as leverage: if the Dakota signed a new treaty, they would get the money owed them. This sticking point led to a breakdown in talks after August 1. As at Traverse des Sioux, it appears Henry Sibley was instrumental in negotiating treaty terms off the record, possibly utilizing his kinship ties and connections within the Dakota community. Somehow, the representatives signed a treaty almost identical to the Traverse des Sioux agreement on August 5, 1851, at Bdote. Wabasha, Ta Oyate Duta, and others tried to negotiate more favorable terms to the end. Commissioner Lea insulted Wabasha and Ta Oyate Duta for resisting, and scolded all the Dakota for taking so much time to deliberate. Lea said to them, "Sensible men among you must know that your Great Father is disposed to treat you fairly; but there are perhaps some bad and foolish men among you who advise you to pursue a different course. You ought to have sense enough to know what is for your good, and sense enough to act accordingly. But if you are not prepared to do so, we have nothing more to say."[85]

Wakute was wary of promises made by the US government. He noted that the Treaty of 1837 had been changed in Washington, DC, and made "very different from what they had been told and all were shamed." Wabasha stood and spoke to the Dakota present. "You have said, young men, that the chief who got up first to sign the treaty you would kill. It is this that has caused the difficulty." The young Dakota men said they had not meant to threaten their leaders but "they didn't like it for the land belongs to the braves." Under unrelenting pressure from the treaty commissioners, the Dakota finally signed, led by Ta Oyate Duta. The Waȟpekute present signed agreements to have payments for debts go directly to certain traders, but the Bdewakaŋtuŋwaŋ refused to do so, preferring to have more control.[86]

In June 1852 Congress ratified the treaties but made two important changes. The US government nullified the reservation as described in the treaties and replaced it with one that the president would decree at a future date. Politicians also changed the language to state that payments would be made directly to the Dakota, as they had been in the 1837 treaty, "unless the imperious interest of the Indian or Indians, or some treaty stipulation, shall require the payment to be made otherwise, under the direction of the President." In September of 1852 trader Henry Rice, working for Ramsey, obtained the signatures of Dakota leaders assenting to the treaty amendments and giving Ramsey power of attorney over the money due the Dakota. Rice did not call general councils of the Dakota, but negotiated with groups of Dakota leaders at Traverse des Sioux and at his store in St. Paul. Rice told the Dakota that the new documents "broke all former papers." Thus, the Dakota left for their fall hunt believing the "traders' paper" was void and their payment would be forthcoming. In October the commissioner of Indian Affairs provided Ramsey with $593,050 to execute the treaties.

When it came time to pay the Dakota late in the fall of 1852, Ramsey used his power of attorney and the vague amendment language to take control of the funds due the Dakota so he could pay the traders directly. He told the Dakota the "traders' paper" was still legally binding and he, as territorial governor, was bound to carry it out. He also tried to get the Dakota to sign receipts as "cumulative evidence" that money passed through their hands, though it never did. Four Waȟpekute leaders signed a receipt, but the Bdewakaŋtuŋwaŋ, Waȟpetuŋwaŋ, and Sisituŋwaŋ resisted. When the Bdewakaŋtuŋwaŋ met Ramsey at Bdote, they demanded their money. When Ramsey told them to pay the traders, Wabasha had enough: "Take it back," he said of the money, "we will take back our land." With cold weather coming, the Bdewakaŋtuŋwaŋ were in need of provisions, and the government withheld their annuities in an effort to pressure them. Ramsey also paid money to Bdewakaŋtuŋwaŋ leaders individually in an attempt to divide them. At the same time, the US Army had confined five Dakota men at Fort Snelling for killing Ojibwe people. Ramsey told the Bdewakaŋtuŋwaŋ leaders their kin would be released once they consented to the direct payment of traders.

When the Waȟpetuŋwaŋ and Sisituŋwaŋ met Ramsey at Traverse des Sioux, they fought his control of the treaty money too. Sisituŋwaŋ leader Maza Ša (Red Iron) led a group of Dakota soldiers to the council and attempted to stop all interactions between his people and Ramsey. In response, Ramsey had soldiers from Fort Snelling occupy the council site and arrest Maza Ša. After seeing Maza Ša arrested and with the cold of winter coming on, the Waȟpetuŋwaŋ and Sisituŋwaŋ finally signed receipts. After forcing the Dakota to relinquish their right to handle the treaty money, Ramsey had it distributed to the traders. Thus, the United States removed the Dakota people from Bdote through manipulation, deceit, coercion, and corruption.[87]

Once again, settler colonists began flooding the land west of the Mississippi before the treaties were ratified. Residents of eastern towns celebrated when news of the treaties reached them. Sibley observed that "people [were] almost crazy to get claims on the west of the Mississippi." Ramsey did nothing to stop the tide of immigrants and was happy to see small towns popping up across the land so recently taken from the Dakota.

The allure of that land was enormous. Thomas Jefferson's vision of the yeoman farmer was central to US national identity. Individual, independent, hardworking farmers would make successful, upstanding, productive citizens. In an agricultural country, owning land was the key to opportunity, and it could bring security and status. Children of farmers in the eastern United States and immigrants from Europe were flooding into the West as fast as lands could be opened, looking to get their own. With rampant speculation, they had to move fast to get it. And when they did, they faced the backbreaking work of building farmsteads and surviving on them through Minnesota's extreme weather, hoping to bring in crops and raise families—thus creating a powerful legacy for their descendants.[88]

Removal of the Dakota to the Minnesota River reservation started in 1853. The Dakota were reluctant to leave their homelands. Only five years later, forces converged to coerce the Dakota to cede half of their new reservation. The tide of colonists spreading up the Minnesota River Valley swelled, and many saw the Dakota reservation as an impediment to progress. Joseph R. Brown, the reservation's

Indian agent, thought the Dakota would not acculturate until their practice of communal land ownership was ended. He believed that if the reservation was reduced in size and the land allotted, the Dakota would be forced to farm. Further, Brown and others remained aware that the 1851 reservation only existed "at the president's pleasure." According to the US legal system, the Dakota could be removed at any time.

In 1858 Brown and others handpicked Dakota leaders and manipulated them into traveling to Washington, DC, with brief mentions that the president simply wanted to discuss the treaties of 1851. Hoping that the US government wanted to right past wrongs, the Dakota agreed. When they arrived, Indian Commissioner Charles Mix met with the Bdewakaŋtuŋwaŋ and Waȟpekute, and then the Sisituŋwaŋ and Wahpeton, much as had been done in 1851. The detailed list of grievances presented by leaders like Ta Oyate Duta was ignored. Mix demanded the Dakota cede half their reservation or lose it all, reminding them they lived on the Minnesota River by the president's whim. With no other options, the Dakota signed the new land cession. "We had, we supposed, made a complete treaty," said Ta Oyate Duta, commenting on the 1851 treaty, "and we were promised a great many things,

The Newcomers

THE MOST COMMON TERM for European Americans who surged into western lands during the nineteenth century is "settlers." The term implies settling empty land, bringing order and civilization, and the inherent right of European Americans to take Indigenous homelands. From the point of view of many native people, European Americans represented exactly the opposite. The newcomers took land that native people had occupied for millennia, replaced order with chaos, and brought waves of displacement and violence. Many historians now describe these European American immigrants by their place of origin or profession in order to avoid using "settler." Indigenous studies scholars have also begun using the term "colonist" or, more specifically, "settler colonist" to describe European Americans who claimed land that was seized from its original inhabitants. "Settler colonists" stay on the land, want Indigenous people to disappear, and found new political orders. "Settler colonialism" can describe the past and the present. For example, under this definition the United States can be defined as a "colonist settler-state."[4] ☾

On a map created by the Bureau of American Ethnology in 1899, Dakota land cessions in southern Minnesota: area marked 243 (in pink), 1837; 289 (orange), 1851; 413 and 414 (pink and yellow), 1858. The area marked 440, in blue, marks the reservation in 1862. *Indian Land Cessions in the United States, compiled by Charles C. Royce and presented as Part 2 of the Eighteenth Annual Report of the Bureau of American Ethnology to the Secretary of the Smithsonian Institution, 1896–97. Printed by the Government Printing Office in 1899.*

horses, cattle, flour, plows, and farming utensils, but now it appears the wind blows it all off and that we got good words and nothing else."[89]

All that was left to the Dakota was a strip of land on the south side of Mni Sota Wakpa that ran for 140 miles and was only ten miles broad. The reservation was divided into two agencies: the Yellow Medicine, or Upper Agency, which served the Sisituŋwaŋ and Wahpeton, and the Redwood, or Lower Agency, which served the Bdewakaŋtuŋwaŋ and Waḣpekute. The land was parceled into eighty-acre allotments for each head of family. The Dakota struggled to practice their traditional lifeways on the small reservation of allotted land; treaty goods and annuities had become essential to their

survival. Hunting parties and small communities traveled and stayed outside the reservation. A limited number of Dakota traveled to the region of Bdote during the 1850s.

Overall, however, the 1851 treaties cut the Dakota off from Bdote. Soldiers stationed at newly constructed Fort Ridgely policed the reservation and for the most part kept the Dakota confined. The US government designed the reservation system to concentrate and control Indigenous people with the aim of "civilizing" them. It was necessary, said Indian Commissioner Luke Lea, that the Dakota "be placed in positions where they can be controlled and finally compelled by stern necessity to resort to agricultural labor or starve."[90]

Three Dakota people at Mniḣaḣa (Minnehaha Falls), 1857. Photograph by Benjamin Franklin Upton.

The Sale of Fort Snelling

By the mid-1850s, changes in society and the economy and territorial expansion of the United States rendered Fort Snelling obsolete. The US Army had achieved its major goals: protecting the fur trade and deterring colonial advances by the British. It had been partially successful in mediating peace between the Dakota and Ojibwe and keeping colonists off Indigenous land until it could be officially acquired by the US government. Now, with the territory formed, the fur trade boom past, the Dakota and some Ojibwe concentrated on reservations, and the fear of threats from European powers waning, Fort Snelling ceased to have a purpose in US expansionist policy. Troops from the fort began ranging farther afield on expeditions into Iowa, into the Red River Valley, and as far west as present-day central Montana. The US Army built forts further west, and half the Fort Snelling garrison moved to Fort Ridgely after it was constructed in 1853.

As early as 1849, there was a proposal to abandon the fort. In 1852, no doubt in response to pressure from those who wanted to develop the land, the borders of the Fort Snelling military reservation were reduced from the large land grab of 1839. Some thought it could become a military academy or asylum. The fort became a tourist destination for visitors and an impediment to city developers. In 1858 local entrepreneur Franklin Steele negotiated a deal with the US secretary of war to purchase the fort and its eight-thousand-acre reserve for $90,000. Fort Snelling was decommissioned, and the US Army garrison marched out on June 1, 1858, less than a month after Minnesota statehood. Steele had hoped to sell lots in his proposed "City of Fort Snelling," but the effects of the financial panic of 1857 dashed his plans. Instead, the fort's parade ground became a pasture for Steele's sheep, and it hosted the second Minnesota State Fair in 1860. Across the river, Mendota assumed new importance when Henry Sibley was elected Minnesota's first state governor. Between 1858 and 1860, Sibley's house at Mendota was the state's first official governor's office.[91]

Fort Snelling during the American Civil War

When the American Civil War began on April 12, 1861, Minnesota governor Alexander Ramsey was lobbying in Washington, DC. He immediately pledged a thousand Minnesota volunteer soldiers to the war effort—the first troops offered to the federal government during the war. The Minnesota adjutant general gained use of Fort Snelling from Franklin Steele, and once again the fort became central to Minnesota history.[92]

At the beginning of the war, Fort Snelling had been neglected for three years, and civilians were hired to make improvements to the original buildings. Troops were housed wherever there was space, but soon facilities at Fort Snelling underwent their first major expansion. The army constructed stockyards, stables, warehouses, and barracks within a large enclosure on the prairie outside the old fort walls. A large military prison was also built outside the walls in 1865.[93]

While at the fort, recruits learned how to be soldiers and spent their time marching, learning the manual of arms, and standing guard duty. As before, many women worked at the fort as laundresses, hospital matrons, and domestic servants. Many of the women were married to soldiers, and the couples' children lived at the post. As the war continued, more federal money flowed into the state, and

civilians visited the post to secure contracts to provide the army with services. Central to much of the business was Franklin Steele, who also worked as the post sutler.[94]

The first troops mustered into service at Fort Snelling on April 29, 1861, and formed the famous First Minnesota Volunteer Infantry Regiment. Throughout the war, Minnesota recruited twenty-one military units totaling about twenty-five thousand soldiers. One hundred four of the Minnesota recruits were African Americans, the majority of whom enlisted at Richfield, St. Paul, and Fort Snelling. When the draft was instituted, some of them served as substitutes for men who did not want to enter the military. African American men served in US Colored Troop units, which were racially segregated; their officers were white men, including 108 from Minnesota. African American Minnesotans served in

many battles, including Nashville, Tupelo, and Petersburg. The creation of these units began the racial segregation of the US armed forces that lasted until 1948. Dakota and Ojibwe men also enlisted in several Minnesota units and served throughout the Civil War.[95]

Minnesota troops played important roles in many major battles of the American Civil War. The First Minnesota Infantry served in the eastern theater of the war, fighting in famous battles like the first battle of Bull Run, Antietam, and Gettysburg. Most of Minnesota's Civil War units, including infantry, artillery, and cavalry, campaigned in the western theater. Minnesotans fought in the western theater battles of Shiloh, Chickamauga, Missionary Ridge, Nashville, and others. When troops returned home from the war, Fort Snelling served as their mustering out point. The First Minnesota was welcomed with a

First Minnesota Mounted Rangers at Fort Snelling, in front of temporary barracks outside fort walls, 1864.

great celebration, but this was not true for all Minnesota veterans. By the summer of 1865, returning soldiers were passing through Fort Snelling and St. Paul without any fanfare. To address this situation, the city set up a soldiers' home and a soldiers' reception committee was established to run "welcome home" festivities. For the rest of 1865, civilians at Fort Snelling, parades, banquets, and triumphal arches greeted those who returned.[96]

The US–Dakota War of 1862

The causes of the US–Dakota War were varied and complex, but taking a broad perspective suggests that the onslaught of colonialism ignited the war. Across the globe and throughout history, many peoples, facing colonization and the loss of their very identity—pushed to the brink—have made one last desperate attempt to resist. The US–Dakota War of 1862 is a dramatic example of this. Many Dakota resented the United States for the treaties of 1851 and 1858, and they suffered from broken promises and ill treatment. More and more, the traditional Dakota way of life was under attack from US colonial policies. Indian agents pushed the Dakota to change the way they lived, withholding goods from those who did not. Some adopted European American forms of agriculture, religion, education, and dress in order to survive. In 1861 the crops on the reservation failed, which led to a winter of near starvation. Food was still scarce on the reservation in 1862, and the late arrival of a shipment of gold, delayed by the Civil War, put off the annual disbursement of annuity payments. The agent preferred to distribute the cash and goods all at once. Starving, the Dakota of the Upper Agency demanded the food held at the agency warehouse, which was to be part of the annuities they were owed. Conflict between the Dakota and the local US Army contingent was narrowly avoided when some Dakota broke into the agency warehouse to obtain food. Tensions on the reservation continued in early August as councils were held between Dakota leaders and the agency traders. Ta Oyate Duta later recalled that storekeeper Andrew Myrick told the Dakota if they were hungry, they could "eat grass or their own dung." The Dakota at the Lower Agency faced a similar situation as traders refused to extend any more credit.[97]

On August 17, 1862, the US–Dakota War began to the north of the Dakota reservation, at Acton Township in Meeker County. Four hungry Dakota hunters, after arguing over eggs stolen from a homestead, killed five European American civilians, then returned to the Lower Sioux Agency to report their action. The Dakota, who made decisions by consensus and who were bound by kinship obligations to support their relatives, were divided on whether to go to war and broke into factions. The heart of the war effort lay with the soldiers' lodge of the Bdewakaŋtuŋwaŋ band led by Šakpedaŋ (Little Six) and spread from there. Bdewakaŋtuŋwaŋ warriors pressured Ta Oyate Duta to lead the war effort. In an impassioned speech, Ta Oyate Duta told them, "See!—the white men are like the locusts when they fly so thick that the whole sky is a snow storm. You may kill one—two—ten, and ten times ten will come to kill you. Count your fingers all day long and white men with guns in their hands will come faster than you can count." Despite his misgivings, Ta Oyate Duta agreed to lead the war effort, concluding, "Ta Oyate Duta is not a coward: he will die with you."[98]

Over the next six weeks, a brutal war engulfed the Minnesota River Valley. Dakota warriors attacked the agencies, and Bdewakaŋtuŋwaŋ war leader Wamditaŋka (Big

Eagle) recalled that Myrick "was lying on the ground dead, with his mouth stuffed full of grass, and the Indians were saying tauntingly: 'Myrick is eating grass himself.'" Dakota warriors attacked homesteads, Fort Ridgely, and New Ulm, and they fought pitched battles with the US Army and citizen militias. Terror spread throughout the Minnesota River Valley as groups of Dakota murdered all the whites they could find, killing entire families, and, as was their practice in war, mutilated some of their remains. Panic engulfed the region and colonists fled east. Many Dakota opposed their relatives, saved colonists from death, and protected them after they were captured. The Dakota who argued for peace occupied a precarious position between the Dakota war faction and the colonist society. The exact number of people who lost their lives will never be known, but it is estimated that the war (and subsequent violence into 1865) resulted in the deaths of an estimated 73 US soldiers and 575 white civilians, including militia, and an unknown number of Dakota (possibly 75 to 100).[99]

Earlier in August, recruitment of the Sixth through Eleventh Infantry regiments meant for service in the Civil War had commenced. When news of the Dakota attacks reached the fort, these units were all in partial states of recruitment, and those soldiers already at Fort Snelling had received little training. Governor Ramsey appointed Henry Sibley a colonel in the state's military forces and commander of the army that would march against the Dakota. Sibley led four hastily armed companies of the Sixth Infantry Regiment from Fort Snelling to St. Peter. Over the next few days, a trickle of supplies and detachments from the other partially recruited infantry regiments and militia units left Fort Snelling to join Sibley.[100]

Governor Ramsey called for swift vengeance on the Dakota before a special session of the state legislature on September 9, 1862: "The Sioux Indians of Minnesota must be exterminated or driven forever beyond the borders of the state." The state's military forces came under federal control on September 16, when Major General John Pope assumed command of the newly created Military Department of the Northwest. Sibley, just appointed a brigadier general of US Army volunteers, directed the US forces in the decisive Battle of Wood Lake on September 23, defeating the Dakota war faction.[101]

Many of the Dakota combatants moved westward into Dakota Territory, while others went north to Canada. But many of the men who had fought stayed with their families, who could not move swiftly enough to escape. Pope, ordering Sibley to press his advance, declared, "It is my purpose utterly to exterminate the Sioux if I have the power to do so and even if it requires a campaign lasting the whole of next year." Sibley, however, sent messengers letting the peaceful Dakota know that his army was advancing and that he did not intend to make war on all the Dakota. He stated that his troops would not harm the peaceful Dakota and those who met his advancing army would be safe. Numerous Dakota who had not participated in the war, as well as some who had, met Sibley's army at a place that came to be called Camp Release. When he arrived, Sibley took the Dakota into the custody of the US military.[102]

Over the course of three weeks, a military commission tried 392 Dakota men for their participation in the war and sentenced 303 of them to death. Some of the trials lasted no longer than five minutes. At the time and ever since, the legal authority of the commission and the procedures it followed have been questioned. As weeks passed, more Dakota voluntarily came to Camp Release, and US patrols captured others. While the Dakota and US soldiers were gathered at Camp Release and the later camp at Lower Agency, measles slowly began to spread through the troops and likely infected the Dakota.[103]

The situation for the Dakota was dire: many settler colonists wanted revenge on all Dakota, regardless of whether they had participated in the war. Winter was approaching, food was scarce, and they were away from their homes on the reservation. On October 7, 1862, General Pope sent orders to Sibley: "I desire you to disarm and send down to Fort Snelling all the Indians, men, women and children, of the Sioux tribe upon whom you can lay your hands. I shall keep and feed for the winter such as are not hung and shot for their crimes, so that with the sanction of Congress obtained this winter they can all be removed beyond the limits of the State, in the spring." Later in October, Pope modified his plans regarding the Dakota and ordered Sibley to send the convicted Dakota to Mankato and the noncombatants to Fort Snelling.[104]

Sibley put Lieutenant Colonel William R. Marshall and three hundred troops of the Eighth and Fifth Minnesota Infantry Regiments in charge of the forced removal of the Dakota from the Minnesota River Valley to Fort Snelling. The Dakota who traveled to Fort Snelling beginning November 7, 1862, numbered 1,658. The vast majority were children, women, and elderly. They followed a northern route, cutting directly east from Lower Sioux across areas with relatively few towns, but the efforts of Colonel Marshall and the military escort could not protect the women and children from a fatal attack in Henderson. US Army scout Samuel J. Brown, son of John R. Brown, stated, "I saw an enraged white woman rush up to one of the wagons and snatch a nursing babe from its mother's breast and dash it violently upon the ground. The soldier's [sic] instantly seized her and led or rather dragged the woman away, and restored the papoose to its mother—limp and almost dead. Although the child was not killed outright, it died a few hours later." Dakota participants recorded other deaths in the oral histories that Dakota families carry to this day. One Dakota family holds the memory of a little girl who witnessed a soldier stab her grandmother on the march. The girl was forced to leave her grandmother behind, and her family never discovered what happened to the elderly woman's body.[105]

The Fort Snelling Concentration Camp

Bdote, the center for so much Dakota spiritual life, would now become the site of pain and despair.

The Dakota noncombatants arrived at Bdote on November 13, 1862, and encamped on the bluff of the Minnesota River about a mile west of Fort Snelling. Shortly after, Marshall and his soldiers moved the Dakota to the river bottom directly below the fort, at the heart of Bdote. Pastor John P. Williamson observed, "They have a guard placed all around the camp all the time to prevent their being abused by whites, and no one is allowed to enter without a pass." But some protectors became attackers. The *Saint Paul Daily Union* reported that a Dakota woman gathering firewood outside the camp was "seized by a number of soldiers and brutally outraged." On December 2 the first census of Dakota at Fort Snelling recorded a total of 1,601 people. There had been a loss of fifty-seven Dakota since they left the Lower Agency on November 7.[106]

In December soldiers built a concentration camp, a wooden stockade over twelve feet high enclosing an area of two or three acres, on the river bottom and moved the Dakota inside its walls. On December 19, 1862, Dakota leaders in the camp sent a petition to the president. In it they described the population of the camp as predominately women and children: "We are here at Fort Snelling, 41 Lower Sioux Indians, 20 Upper Sioux Indians, and about 1,500

Concentration camp at Fort Snelling, 1862–63.

Concentration Camps

A CONCENTRATION CAMP, according to the US Holocaust Memorial Museum, is a "camp in which people are detained or confined, usually under harsh conditions and without regard to legal norms of arrest and imprisonment that are acceptable in a constitutional democracy." The term was first used in the Second Boer War (1899–1902), when the British army confined tens of thousands of Boer and African civilians, mostly women and children, in inadequate camps where many thousands died.

The use of the term for the Dakota camp at Bdote is vigorously disputed at times because of its association with Nazi forced labor and death camps in Europe during World War II. While this association is strong, a concentration camp is not the same as a forced labor or death camp. "Internment camp," sometimes proposed as an option, is defined by the *Oxford English*

Dictionary as "a camp in which prisoners of war, enemy aliens, political prisoners, etc., are detained without trial." The Dakota were not considered prisoners of war and were not political prisoners. The US government did not have a consistent policy concerning Indigenous sovereignty in the nineteenth century, thus "enemy alien" cannot be definitively applied to the Dakota noncombatants. The US government used "internment camp" for the camps that imprisoned Japanese Americans during World War II, but historians and descendants have successfully argued to call them "concentration camps."

The stockade at Bdote was a concentration camp—a place where civilians were confined, in poor conditions, without regard to legal norms of arrest.[5] ☾

women and children and 20 half breed men." A warehouse just outside the camp was used as a hospital and mission station. Throughout the camp's existence, soldiers of the Sixth, Seventh, and Tenth Minnesota Volunteer Infantry Regiments guarded the stockade, controlling movement in and out.[107]

The administration of the camp fell under the authority of Colonel William Crooks, commandant of Fort Snelling. His immediate superior was Sibley, then in command of the Minnesota District of the Northwest Department, with headquarters in St. Paul. Pope remained in command of the entire Northwest Department. The US Army and the Department of the Interior fought over whose responsibility it was to maintain the camp. The Department of the Interior's Office of Indian Affairs had administered the Minnesota River reservation. Pope and Sibley contended that it was the department's responsibility to pay for the upkeep of the concentration camp. Pope wanted "the government to feed and clothe [the Dakota] cheaply, and for that purpose to use the annuities now paid, and the proceeds of the sale of their reservations." Interior Department officials, angered by previous insults from Pope and his decision to take the Dakota into custody, refused to do so.[108]

Faced with a limited military budget, Sibley and his superiors decided that feeding the Dakota full army rations was not necessary. In addition, the army decided the Dakota were not prisoners of war, and therefore could be fed at the army's discretion. The army fed

the Dakota bread, hardtack, flour, beef, and pork—foodstuffs that made up the typical army ration. The meat provided by the army was sometimes of poor quality, and the quantity of food was not always sufficient.[109]

Conditions in the camp added to the misery. Temperatures fluctuated above and below freezing, and the ground became unsanitary as offal mixed with the mud. TiWakaŋ (Sacred Lodge, also known as Gabriel Renville) recounted, "we were so crowded and confined that an epidemic broke out among us and the children were dying day and night." The Dakota had little immunity to the measles virus, most of them having never encountered it before, and the disease swept through the camp; it also hit groups of European American refugees who had crowded into towns after fleeing the war.

It is estimated that between 130 and 300 Dakota people died over the winter of 1862–63, mainly due to measles and other diseases. Wicaŋȟpi Waśte Wiŋ (Good Star Woman) recounted decades later, through intermediaries, "All of the children had measles. . . . Sometimes 20 to 50 died in a day and were buried in a long trench, the old, large people underneath and the children on top." Stephen Riggs, a missionary to the Dakota, observed the horror in the camp: "Since the Dakota Camp has been placed at Fort Snelling, quite a number have died of measles and other diseases. I learn that their buried dead have been taken up and mutilated. They are now keeping their dead or burying them in their teepees." Riggs wrote further, "It is a very sad place now. The crying hardly ever stops. From five to ten die daily." The *Saint Paul Daily Press* recorded the efforts of some Dakota to bury their dead on Oheyawahe: "A number of papooses have died during the winter of infantile diseases and were usually buried in an old burial ground back of Mendota."[110]

Without land, employment, or annuities, the Dakota had no way to provide for

themselves, and some European Americans found opportunities to exploit them. Williamson noted, "[The Dakota] can earn nothing. They have been deprived of their arms and implements of hunting. With very few exceptions, their horses, cattle and wagons were lost or have been disposed of to supply their urgent wants, and they have nothing remaining except their cooking utensils, tents, and clothes on their backs which will soon be worn out." Businessmen like Franklin Steele took economic advantage of the camp's inhabitants. Steele obtained the contract to supply rations to the camp, and he also opened a sutler store in the camp to sell supplemental food and other items. Many of the prisoners of Dakota and European American ancestry owned scrip they had received from previous treaties. These certificates entitled the bearer to up to 640 acres of unsurveyed federal land in exchange for land given up in treaties. Some who possessed scrip sold it to Franklin Steele and others in order to supplement the military-issue rations they received.

The army permitted US civilians to enter the camp as cultural tourists. Photographers took pictures of Dakota men, women, and children, and made money off the images in the popular carte de visite market. Tourists treated the Dakota as less than human, opening tipi doors to gawk at them. Several missionaries visited the camp, pressing their faith on the Dakota. Vulnerable, held captive, surrounded by death and armed soldiers, many Dakota converted to Christianity while in the camp. More Dakota converted to Christianity in 1862 than had since missionaries arrived in the 1830s. Some missionaries questioned how genuine or pragmatic these conversions were.[111]

While the Dakota families suffered at Fort Snelling, the army held more than three hundred Dakota men at Mankato. President Abraham Lincoln approved the execution of thirty-eight Dakota men, found guilty by the tribunal of rape and participating in "massacres," and they were hanged at Mankato on December 26, 1862. It was the largest mass execution in US history. The remaining Dakota men, still sentenced to death, continued to languish in the Mankato jail.[112]

Throughout the winter, the US Congress considered bills to remove the Dakota from their homeland. On February 16, 1863, Congress passed an act that "abrogated and annulled" all treaties with the Dakota people. The act also stated that all lands held by the Dakota, and all annuities due to them, were forfeited to the US government. A second bill, providing for the removal of the Dakota from their ancestral homelands, passed on March 3, 1863. The aftermath of the US–Dakota War of 1862 also engulfed the Ho-Chunk, who were living at Blue Earth in southern Minnesota at the time of the war. Settler colonists' desire to remove all Indians from Minnesota led to a similar bill to evict the Ho-Chunk, who had been uninvolved in the war but resided on prime agricultural land that US citizens wished to obtain. In northern Minnesota, a major altercation between the Ojibwe and the United States that coincided with the US–Dakota War almost turned violent. Led by Bagone-giizhig (Hole in the Day), a group of Ojibwe, angered by annuity thefts and the unwanted recruitment of Ojibwe men for military service, gutted European American missions, trading posts, and homesteads. War was avoided; the US government acceded to the Ojibwe's demands and made no attempt to remove them from the state.

Just over two weeks after the Dakota and Ho-Chunk removal bills passed, the concentration camp at Fort Snelling flooded. The army moved the Dakota into another stockade on the river bluff about a mile west of the fort.[113]

Removal of the Dakota, the "Pilgrims," and the Punitive Expeditions

In the spring of 1863 three groups of marginalized people moved through Fort Snelling at Bdote: the Dakota captives, the Ho-Chunk people, and groups of free African Americans.

After the spring thaw opened the rivers, the US government set out to exile the Dakota from Bdote and Mni Sota Makoce as quickly as possible. On April 23, 1863, a steamer carrying the Dakota men who had been held through the winter at Mankato docked briefly at Fort Snelling. The prisoners of the Fort Snelling camp thronged the levee, hoping to reunite with their husbands, fathers, and brothers. After a few dozen Dakota men who had been found not guilty of participating in the war were put ashore, the steamer pulled away, to the distress of families who had no idea if they would ever be reunited. The Dakota men were transported to a prison in Davenport, Iowa, where at least 120 of them died.

In early May the army put the Dakota captives from the Fort Snelling camp aboard steamers and took them to a desolate reservation at Crow Creek, Dakota Territory. Some Dakota people who were connected with traders and missionaries, or able to find work with the army, managed to stay in Minnesota. A group of Dakota men who entered the US Army as scouts served in western Minnesota, while their families stayed on at Fort Snelling, Fort Ridgely, and Camp Pope. A second group of just over thirty Dakota went to Faribault. A final group of fifteen went to Mendota, where Sibley provided them with town lots. The removal of the Ho-Chunk people coincided with that of the Dakota. For a brief time, the US army held hundreds of Ho-Chunk at Fort Snelling before they, too, were removed from the state.[114]

One of the steamers that would remove the Dakota brought free African Americans to Bdote. A preacher named Robert Hickman led a group of about seventy-five men, women, and children who had escaped slavery in Boone Country, Missouri, and called themselves Pilgrims. Accounts suggest the Pilgrims obtained their freedom by running away; it is also possible US troops serving in the Civil War emancipated them. Over seventy years later, Robert Hickman's son, John, provided the only eyewitness account: "The preacher, aided by fellow enslaved people, began the secret construction of a flat river boat. After endless nights of tireless labor, the boat was completed and preparations were made to gather their families and flee. On a dark, moonless night, families and simple provisions were quickly tucked in the stern of the boat and the departure was underway. No oars, no sails, no means of motivation, the fleeing families, led by Hickman, raised their faces heavenward and prayed and sang hymns, tirelessly, endlessly." The Pilgrims drifted down the Missouri River and entered the Mississippi. There, a northbound steamer captain encountered them and "tied a strong towing-cable to the floundering boat and resumed his journey northward."

There was a labor shortage in Minnesota, and Henry Sibley had been seeking to use "contrabands"—people who had escaped slavery during the Civil War—to work as teamsters. The army was preparing for expeditions into Dakota Territory to kill or capture the Dakota who had fled west after the war. Sibley could not spare men from the ranks to work as teamsters, and he saw "contrabands" as a cheap and willing labor force. Hickman and the Pilgrims were one of multiple groups of recently freed African Americans brought to Minnesota in the spring of 1863.

When the steamboat carrying the Pilgrims arrived at St. Paul, local police and recent immigrants argued against letting the African Americans into town. The police called

Department of Dakota

In 1866 the US military created the Department of Dakota, which encompassed Minnesota, Dakota Territory, and much of Montana Territory, and placed its headquarters at Fort Snelling. The army constructed forts throughout the territories, expanding the reach of the United States into the land purchased from France in 1803—the land of the Oceti Šakowiŋ and other Indigenous peoples. In 1871 Franklin Steele filed a claim for $162,000 against the government, seeking to be paid for the US Army's use of the fort during the Civil War. However, Steele still owed money on the original purchase price, so a deal was struck. The

Headquarters of the Department of Dakota, about 1890.

government kept fifteen hundred acres of the military reservation and gave sixty-four hundred back to Steele. The department headquarters was moved to St. Paul in 1867, then back to the fort around 1876. General Alfred Terry commanded the department but kept his offices in St. Paul.

Former Minnesota governor and senator Alexander Ramsey served as secretary of war under President Rutherford B. Hayes from 1879 to 1881, and he made sure ample funds were appropriated for Fort Snelling. Congress approved appropriations and paid for the construction of a row of officers' houses, a department headquarters, and several other buildings. The additions became known as the Upper Post and the area of the original fort was called the Lower Post. In 1880 a bridge was built across the Mississippi linking the fort to St. Paul. In the 1880s the old fort barracks and frame buildings were still used, but

they began to deteriorate and the walls were demolished.[121]

Through these years, the cities in the area of Bdote were growing, and the newcomers who built them had little or no concern about places that were sacred to the Dakota. The story of *Fort Snelling at Bdote* becomes a deeply military one—a story of Fort Snelling, growing outside the walls of the original diamond and across the military reservation, and not of Bdote. The colonial society that had built Fort Snelling believed the Dakota were gone; the story of Bdote was in effect suppressed. But Dakota families continued to live at Faribault and Mendota and in the other Dakota communities of the state; Dakota people continued to visit Mni Sni and Oheyawahe and Owamniyomni. Although their stories have less prominence in the next several decades of the area's military history, the Dakota never left Bdote.

By the 1870s, new buildings outside the fort walls extended west across the bluff, and a railroad bridge and dike, built directly across Bdote, caused flooding on the Minnesota River.

Company I of the African American Twenty-Fifth Infantry at Fort Snelling, 1883.

Buffalo Soldiers

In November of 1882 elements of the segregated, all–African American Twenty-Fifth Infantry arrived at Fort Snelling.

The segregation of the US Army began during the American Civil War. Afterward, six segregated regiments were organized from US Colored Troop units. In 1869 these six units were reduced to four segregated Regular Army units: the Twenty-Fourth and Twenty-Fifth Infantry Regiments, and the Ninth and Tenth Cavalry Regiments. The army stationed these units mostly in the western United States, where they garrisoned posts and campaigned against Indigenous peoples. While fighting the Tenth Cavalry, American Indians—either Cheyenne or Comanche or Apache, or perhaps all three groups—called them "Buffalo Soldiers." The exact origin of the name is unclear, but stories point to the soldiers' curly

hair, their bravery in battle, or their use of buffalo robes in winter as reasons for the moniker. Eventually the name became synonymous with all of the segregated regiments.[122]

Fort Snelling was the regimental headquarters of the Twenty-Fifth Infantry until May 1888. During the unit's tenure, several companies and the regimental band garrisoned the fort. The rest of the regiment garrisoned Fort Hale on the Missouri River and Fort Meade, just north of the Black Hills in Dakota Territory. The troops in the West spent their time protecting US assets in the region, constructing roads, repairing telegraph lines, and policing American Indians confined on the Red Cloud Agency and the Crow Creek Reservation.

Back in Minnesota, companies at Fort Snelling performed garrison duty. Members of the unit, like all other soldiers who served at the fort, could take leave in nearby St. Paul and Minneapolis. The regimental band, however, saw more of Minnesota. In 1883 and 1884 the band played at commencement ceremonies of the military school in Faribault. Also in 1883 the band performed at the Minnesota State Fair held in Rochester. The Twenty-Fifth was deployed to posts further west in Montana Territory in 1888. A few veterans of the unit decided to make their homes in Minneapolis after their enlistments ended.[123]

Wars of Imperialism

By the late nineteenth century, the United States claimed territory across North America from the Atlantic Ocean to the Pacific, forming a contiguous empire of settlers. Coming into its own as a powerful industrial nation, the country worked to spread its influence and become a world power. These imperial ambitions led to military conflicts in Cuba and the Philippines. Like the nation, Fort Snelling expanded physically, and troops stationed there went abroad to fight in wars for empire.

In 1889 the Third US Infantry arrived at Fort Snelling, and beginning in the 1890s many stone and brick structures were built on the military reservation to accommodate units of infantry, cavalry, and artillery. When the Spanish-American War began in 1898, the Third Infantry departed for service in Cuba. Elements of the Third fought in the battles of El Caney, San Juan Hill, and Santiago de Cuba. The Third returned from Cuba in September 1898. The Treaty of Paris signed in 1898 ended the Spanish-American War, and in it, the Spanish ceded territories to the United States, including the Philippines. The Philippine Republic rejected the treaty and eventually declared war on the United States. On January 30, 1899, the regiment left Fort Snelling for service in the Philippine-American War (1899–1902). For much of its first year, the Third saw combat and active duty. From late 1899 to early 1902, the unit guarded important points and railways at San Fernando, Caloocan, and Manila. Skirmishes with Philippine soldiers were frequent and the colonization of Filipino lands was brutal. Over the course of the Third's tour of duty, 593 Minnesotans served in its ranks. After its stint in the Philippines, the Third did not return to Fort Snelling until 1921.[124]

After the Philippine-American War, Fort Snelling was designated a brigade-level post, housing infantry, artillery, and cavalry troops. The military continued to build new buildings and make infrastructure improvements, including an electrical plant, and the old buildings of the lower post were modified to the Spanish Mission style architecture for a time.[125]

Spanish war recruits occupied tents near the new brick barracks on Taylor Avenue, about 1898.

The Battle of Sugar Point

Soldiers from Fort Snelling took part in one last battle with Indigenous people in the 1890s. At that time, US authorities frequently arrested Ojibwe people in northern Minnesota for trivial causes—or seized them as witnesses—and transported them far off their reservations to Duluth or Minneapolis for trial. Further damaging Ojibwe–US relations, logging companies were illegally taking lumber from the Leech Lake Reservation, and leaders of the Pillager Band of Ojibwe formally protested the theft.

In April of 1898 Bagone-giizhig (Hole in the Day), a sixty-two-year-old Ojibwe man, was charged with bootlegging and transported to Duluth. Freed for lack of evidence, he was left to make his way back home—more than 130 miles—on foot. On September 15, 1898, Bagone-giizhig and Zhaaboondeshkang (He Who Treads Through the Center) were at the Onigum Agency to receive their annuity payments when a US deputy marshal again seized them in relation to a bootlegging trial. Bagone-giizhig seems to have been determined not to be arrested again. Aided by their kin, the two Ojibwe men resisted arrest and fled. Over the course of several weeks, US authorities tried to force Bagone-giizhig and others implicated in the resistance to surrender, but they refused.

General John A. Bacon, acting commander of the Department of Dakota, and seventy-seven men of the Third Infantry made their way from Fort Snelling to Sugar Point with the goal of capturing Bagone-giizhig and the Ojibwe who had helped him resist. After scouring the point and making some arrests, the Third Infantry assembled in a clearing. Accounts differ on how the battle began, but the troops came under fire from Ojibwe who believed their people were under attack. US casualties from the battle were six killed and ten wounded. There were also civilian casualties: one Ojibwe policeman was killed, and at least four other civilians were wounded. Eventually the commissioner of Indian Affairs arrived and held a council with the Ojibwe. Those who had warrants for their arrest agreed to surrender and served brief prison terms in Duluth. Bagone-giizhig did not participate in the fighting and was never apprehended. The Ojibwe who fought at Sugar Point were never arrested either. The Third Infantry returned to Fort Snelling, where funerals were held for those who had been killed. The Battle at Sugar Point was one of the last battles fought between Indigenous peoples and US military forces.[126]

Fort Snelling during World War I

In the 1910s Fort Snelling was a mobilization point for National Guard units sent to protect the border with Mexico during the Mexican Revolution. When the United States entered World War I in April 1917, the fort became an induction and processing center for thousands of recruits. The army renovated the post to prepare it for expanded service, building a temporary cantonment of several wooden buildings at the present location of the Minneapolis–St. Paul International Airport, and the YMCA enlarged its facilities at the post. The fort's large brick barracks became a training school for junior officers, and they hosted two successive officer training camps. Over four thousand men enrolled in the camp and more than twenty-five hundred became officers. Training focused on military science, physical fitness, and drill. The military used the terrain of Bdote for maneuvers, and several mock "battles of Pilot Knob" were fought on Oheyawahe.[127]

In September 1918, after the training of officers ended, Fort Snelling was designated General Hospital 29 and came under the auspices of the Medical Department of the US Army. Existing structures were remodeled and several new buildings were constructed. Beginning in a single base building, the hospital came to embrace the entire Fort Snelling military post and twelve hundred beds by the time it closed on August 1, 1919. The hospital staff's first major duty was caring for victims of the 1918 influenza pandemic. After the pandemic subsided, workers at the hospital began treating veterans returning home from World War I.

The hospital became a "reconstruction hospital," as 80 percent of its work was surgical: general surgery, orthopedics, dental work, eye, ear, nose, and throat treatments, and nerve surgery. The staff took pride in their pioneering orthopedic work and customized every artificial limb for its wearer. The medical service at the hospital also treated soldiers who returned home with illnesses and infections.

Officer candidates practicing bayonet drill at Fort Snelling, about 1918.

Aides in occupational therapy at General Hospital Number 29, Fort Snelling, 1918.

The hospital's educational service department, with a staff of eighty, provided instruction in academic subjects, woodworking, automobile and tractor repair, driving, agriculture, music, and crafts. The educational service was seen as an integral part of "reconstruction." The education did not provide any vocational certificate but was meant to meet soldiers' interests or help them recover from injuries.

OPPOSITE
Wounded soldiers learning crafts, Fort Snelling hospital, 1918.

An Army Nurse Corps, staffed by women from towns across Minnesota, carried out much of the work at the hospital. The nurses worked as "reconstruction aides," helping with surgery and fitting soldiers with orthopedics. They did most of the educational work and ran therapeutic and recreational programs. From curing fevers to playing board games with victims of "shell shock" (now known as post-traumatic stress disorder, or PTSD), the army nurses cared for their patients in numerous ways. The hospital's publication, *Reveille,* noted, "When the mind is happy and the hands are busily employed nature is helped in her healing process which surgeon and nurse are endeavoring to speed along."

The Red Cross, YMCA, and Knights of Columbus also helped in the rehabilitation. The Red Cross sought to support the hospital's work and provided entertainment for the men. It ran a convalescent house where disabled veterans recovered and a gymnasium to keep up the morale of able-bodied soldiers. The Red Cross also ran an on-post bank and provided the men with luxury items the army could not. By 1918 the Fort Snelling YMCA post had existed for a decade. Its staff and volunteers provided the recovering soldiers with a library and sometimes transported them to the Twin Cities for entertainments. The Knights of Columbus, a Catholic fraternal organization, played an important role in the educational work at the fort. The organization maintained a "home-like club room" with a piano, Victrola player, library books, and magazines. The Knights hosted boxing matches and vaudeville shows in the gym and took hundreds of wounded men on trips to the Twin Cities.[128]

The Country Club of the Army

The decades of peace between World Wars I and II brought an eased atmosphere to Fort Snelling. Polo matches, concerts, parades, athletic contests, and horse and military shows were common occurrences on the military reservation. The fort hosted the Northwest Polo Tournament for several years, beginning in 1923. Soldiers put on military shows to raise money for fellow soldiers in need. A trick horse named Whiskey became a legendary mascot, and the high society of the Twin Cities turned out to see him at civilian horse shows. Units that garrisoned the post began a tradition of winter and summer athletic competitions. Tennis courts, a golf course, and a swimming pool were added to the fort's facilities. A wild game sanctuary was even established on the reserve, and a hunting club complete with hounds ranged across the sanctuary.[129]

Congress reorganized the army with the passage of a new National Defense Act in 1920. The act divided the army into three components: the Regular Army, the National Guard, and the Organized Reserve. The Regular Army units that garrisoned Fort Snelling began a training program for soldiers in the National Guard and Reserves in 1921. That same year the fort also hosted its first Civilian Military Training School (CMTS). The purpose of the CMTS was to "bring together young men of all types, both native and foreign born; to develop closer national and social unity, to teach privileges, duties, and responsibilities of American citizenship." For one month each summer, young men from across the Midwest were trained by army officers. They sat through military science lectures, drilled in the manual of arms, marched, trained with weapons, completed athletic training, and participated in military ceremonies. Between 1921 and 1928 the post trained an estimated fifteen thousand young men.[130]

Soldiers, community organizations, and businesses raised money to build a new chapel on the post. Built by soldiers out of salvaged materials from the 1880 Mississippi River Bridge, it was completed in 1928. The Fort Snelling Chapel, the first nondenominational military post chapel and the first to be funded by public subscription, is still in service.[131]

In the mid-1930s members of the Grand Army of the Republic, Spanish-American War Veterans, Veterans of Foreign Wars, Disabled American Veterans, Jewish War Veterans, and the American Legion came together to push for the establishment of a national military cemetery at Fort Snelling. In 1936 and 1937 Congress approved of the project and passed laws that allowed the secretary of war to set aside a portion of the Fort Snelling military reservation for the cemetery. The national cemetery was dedicated on July 14, 1939. George H. Mallon of Minneapolis was the first person buried in the cemetery. Mallon was a graduate of the Fort Snelling officers training camp, a World War I veteran, and a Medal of Honor recipient. Burials from previous Fort Snelling cemeteries, dating back to the 1820s, were also moved to the national cemetery.[132]

Fort Snelling during World War II

After the bombing of Pearl Harbor on December 7, 1941, the United States entered World War II. Once again, Fort Snelling became a processing center for military recruits and draftees. The fort's facilities expanded to three hundred buildings, which housed and provisioned about three hundred thousand men and women who passed through Fort

Snelling during the war. At its height in 1942, the reception center could process eight hundred recruits per day. Prospective soldiers received medical examinations and vaccinations, took the Army General Classification Test, and were interviewed about their skills, education, and work history. The results of these tests determined their assignments. The recruits mustered into the armed forces and received uniforms. Most recruits spent a short time at Fort Snelling before being shipped to other facilities for basic training. The recruits included African Americans, who served their country despite institutionalized racism in the military and society. Dakota, Ojibwe, and other Indigenous people were also among the trainees who passed through Fort Snelling. American Indians have a long tradition of military service, and they volunteered in disproportionate numbers during World War II.

An electric streetcar called the Fort Snelling Dummy linked the lower and upper posts of the expansive military base. Soldiers could also ride streetcars into Minneapolis and St. Paul. In their free time, soldiers attended dances and socials, golfed, went swimming, and spent time at the post theater and library. To the west of Fort Snelling, Wold-Chamberlain Airport was almost totally taken over by military operations.

In addition to traditional recruits, the military trained specialized units at Fort Snelling. The Ninety-Ninth Infantry Battalion (Separate), which eventually became part of the 474th Infantry, was made up of men who spoke Norwegian. They trained on skis and snowshoes during the Minnesota winters and traveled to Colorado to train in mountain environments—but there was no invasion of Norway, and the unit's soldiers fought as infantryman

A page from the Fort Snelling reception center processing pamphlet, about 1943.

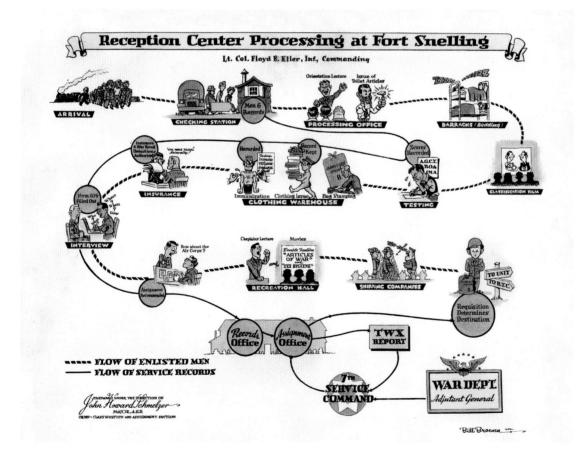

OPPOSITE
Soldiers of the Ninety-Ninth
Infantry training on skis,
1942.

in Europe. The Norwegian-speaking soldiers reached Norway at the end of the war and processed German soldiers who had surrendered.

In 1941 Fort Snelling became the headquarters of the Military Railway Service. Major railway companies sponsored these units, and civilian railway workers helped train them. Trainees also studied maps of foreign railway systems. Units that trained at Fort Snelling served in North Africa in 1943, taking over captured lines. The headquarters of the Military Railway Service was eventually transferred overseas. In addition, the fort was a training center for military police.[133]

As war with Japan threatened, some military officers realized that there would be a need for Japanese linguists and intelligence workers trained in the Japanese language. As a result, the Fourth Army Intelligence School was established in San Francisco in 1941. The school primarily recruited second-generation Japanese Americans, called Nisei. Among the Nisei were a group called Kibei—Japanese Americans who had received education in Japan. Students learned to read and write in Japanese, as well as interrogation and translation skills, document analysis, geography, and map reading. There were lessons on the

Fort Snelling, 1945.

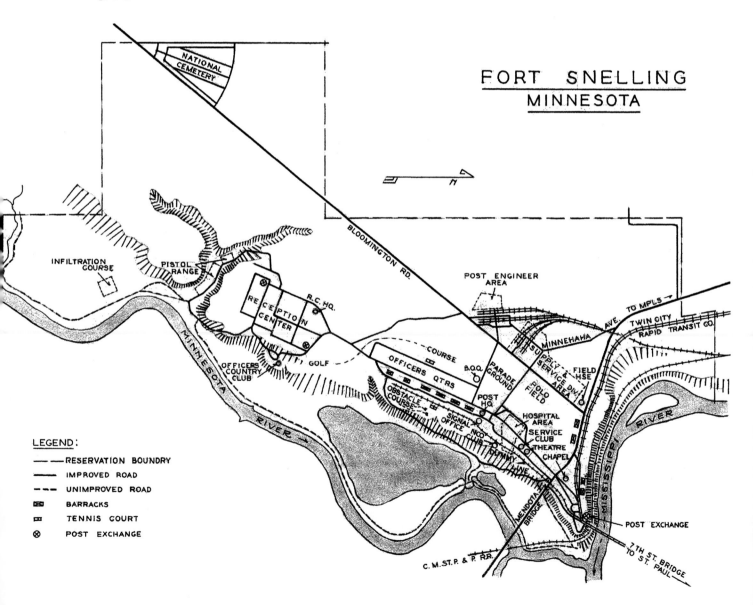

FORT SNELLING
MINNESOTA

LEGEND:

— — — RESERVATION BOUNDRY
———— IMPROVED ROAD
– – – UNIMPROVED ROAD
▨ BARRACKS
▯ TENNIS COURT
⊗ POST EXCHANGE

structure of the Japanese military and Japanese politics and society.

In February 1942 President Franklin D. Roosevelt issued Executive Order 9066, forcing the relocation of many Japanese Americans from the West Coast to concentration camps in the interior of the country. The order prompted the intelligence school to move as well. The head of the school conducted a nationwide survey and eventually met with Minnesota governor Harold Stassen. The school moved to Minnesota because, said the school's commandant, the state "not only had room physically but also had room in the people's hearts." In June the school moved to Camp

Savage in Scott County and was renamed the Military Intelligence Service Language School (MISLS).

After the move to Camp Savage, many of the school's students were recruited from concentration camps. The school population outgrew the post and moved to Fort Snelling in August 1944. After Germany's defeat in May 1945, activity at the school increased, and students began intercepting and translating Japanese radio messages and communiqués directly.

After Japan surrendered, the MISLS grew again, as more linguists were needed for the occupation of Japan. In early 1946 the school

Military Intelligence Service Language School students, 1945.

FORT SNELLING AT BDOTE

was at its largest, with three thousand students. A Women's Army Corps detachment was added, and Korean and Chinese language sections were created. The last class graduated at Fort Snelling in June 1946, and shortly afterward the school moved back to California. Following the war, having been relocated and having had their property liquidated, many Japanese Americans had nothing to go home to. Some decided to make a new life in Minnesota because of their experience at the MISLS. The Japanese American population in the state had grown from fifty-one in 1940 to 1,049 in 1950. "People looked upon you as being a US army soldier, an American citizen," remembered Bud Nakasone, one of the linguists from Hawaii who stayed in Minnesota. "This is what has kept me here for all these years, despite the cold."[134]

The school graduated more than six thousand linguists, roughly 85 percent of whom were Nisei. Graduates had a wide range of experiences. Early students became instructors at the MISLS. Most graduates served in the Pacific or China-Burma-India theaters. There, they communicated with Japanese soldiers, gathered and translated documents, and engaged in combat. Nisei served on the staff of US generals and worked as translators during high-level negotiations. The linguists served in every branch of the military and supported more than 130 wartime organizations.

During the war, graduates of the MISLS worked in secrecy when deployed due to the importance of their mission. It was not until the 1970s, when World War II military intelligence documents were declassified, that their story became public. The intelligence the MISLS graduates provided had been extremely useful. Major General Charles Willoughby, chief of intelligence in the Pacific theater during World War II, credited the Nisei linguists with shortening the war in the East by two years, saving nearly a million lives and billions of dollars.[135]

Decommissioning of Fort Snelling

After World War II, the US military reassessed its assets and decided that Fort Snelling was no longer strategically important. The expansion of the Veterans Administration and Wold-Chamberlain Airport (renamed Minneapolis–St. Paul International Airport in 1948) put pressure on the military reservation, as did urban growth. The fort was also not conducive to divisional level and combined arms training, which the army used at the time. These pressures brought a swift end to the US military's operation of Fort Snelling. Soldiers lowered the flag for the last time on October 14, 1946, after more than 120 years of service. After its second and final decommissioning, the military reservation and the remains of the original fort passed to the Veterans Administration. Much of the original fort had been demolished, and the 1820s buildings that remained had been heavily renovated. Reserve military units operated out of federal offices at the site in subsequent decades.[136]

The military presence at the confluence continued at the national cemetery as well. After World War II, soldiers who had died overseas were buried in the national cemetery at Fort Snelling. Many burials took place between 1947 and 1948 as the federal government worked to reinter soldiers killed in combat overseas. The cemetery became the final resting place for veterans of the Korean and Vietnam wars, as well. In the 1960s additional land was transferred to the national cemetery, bringing its size to 436 acres. In the twenty-first century, veterans of the wars in Iraq and Afghanistan began to be buried there. The cemetery is the final resting place of more than 180,000 servicemen and -women.[137]

Owamniyomni, about 1912.

Indian Mounds Boulevard and the creation of Indian Mounds Park. The mounds that survived became the centerpiece of Indian Mounds Park. Over the decades, archaeologists, city workers, and looters who dug into the mounds found grave goods, seashell beads, and the burials of approximately fifty people. These depredations were formally outlawed in 1976, when the Minnesota legislature passed a law protecting all burials outside of platted cemeteries. Archaeologists and city workers surveyed and rehabilitated the park in the 1980s and 1990s. The only known surviving artifacts from the mounds are now held by the Minnesota Historical Society in compliance with the Native American Graves Protection and Repatriation Act of 1990.[140]

Below the mounds, Wakaŋ Tipi faced a similar fate. St. Paul was the head of practical navigation on the Mississippi, and the area at the foot of the bluffs became a railroad yard where goods brought upstream on steamboats were offloaded and sent on to supply the immigrants colonizing the West. In the decades following the Dakota removal, natural erosion of the limestone cliff sealed the cave. In 1913 a local businessman reopened the cave, looking to exploit it as a tourist destination, and he brought in Blackfeet people from Montana to provide an air of authenticity. His scheme failed; over the decades, squatters lived there, until natural erosion sealed the cave once again.[141]

Across the river and upstream, farmers overtook portions of Oheyawahe. In 1928 Freemasons established Acacia Cemetery on the hill and flattened the hill's knob during its development. As cemetery workers started digging graves, they disturbed Indigenous burials. Some of these remains were reportedly housed at the cemetery mortuary for reburial, but it is not clear what happened to them.[142]

The Creation of Historic Fort Snelling

The idea of preserving Fort Snelling dates back to the 1860s, as the military began to modify the original buildings within the diamond. By the turn of the century, the walls that had formed the old fort's perimeter had collapsed and only four buildings remained: the commandant's house, the officers' quarters, the round tower, and the hexagonal tower. In 1938 the round tower was converted into a museum with funds from the Works Progress Administration. The museum provided an interpretation typical of the time, focusing on the US Army and the familiar story of settlers on the frontier. Murals depicted the Fifth Infantry, Indian Agent Taliaferro negotiating with the Dakota and Ojibwe people, the fur trade, and the arrival of immigrants.[143]

In 1956 the Minnesota Highway Department announced plans to build Highway 55 through the remains of the original fort, encircling the round tower with a cloverleaf.

Widespread public opposition brought that plan to a halt. With the approach of the statehood centennial in 1958, state officials and members of the public were becoming more historically aware, and their opposition to the highway became support for the site's preservation. The highway department rerouted Highway 55 through a covered trench under the fort site. The Daughters of the American Revolution and the Daughters of the Founders and Patriots began raising money for the restoration of Fort Snelling.[144]

In 1957 the Minnesota Statehood Centennial Commission made a grant of $25,000 to the Minnesota Historical Society for archaeological work to uncover the remains of Fort Snelling's original 1820s buildings. On May 11, 1958—the statehood centennial—a refreshed museum opened in the round tower, featuring archaeological artifacts and a focus on military and pioneer history. The public and students

Aerial view of the confluence, 1951. Highway 5 (West Seventh Street) crosses the Mississippi River and cuts through the center of the Fort Snelling diamond and intersects the road to the Fort Snelling–Mendota Bridge, built in 1924–26. The commandant's house, the short barracks, the round tower, and the cavalry barracks are at center right.

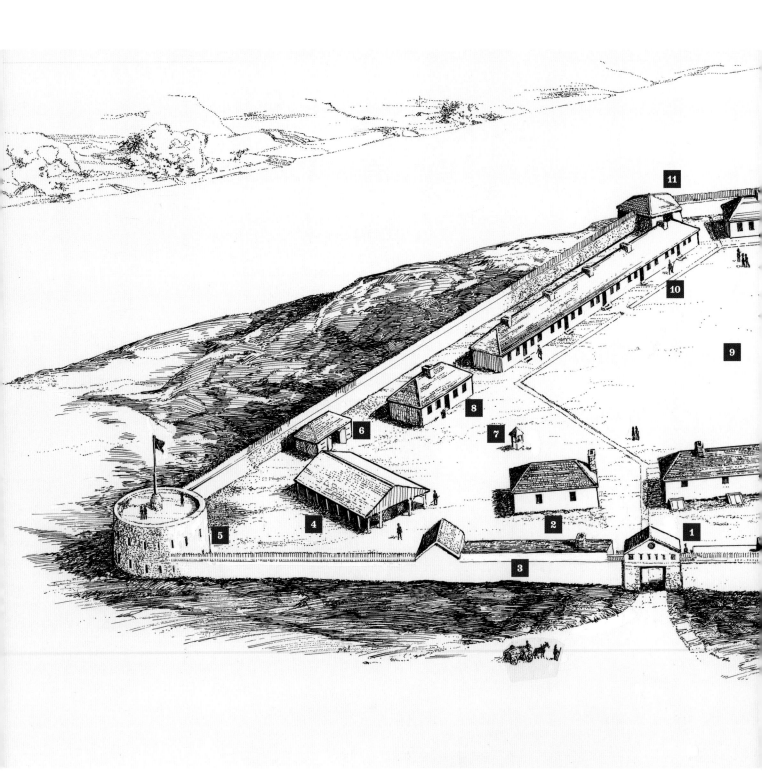

**Restored
Fort Snelling**

1. Gatehouse
2. School
3. Guardhouse
4. Magazine
5. Round tower
6. Gun shed
7. Well

8. Sutler's store
9. Parade ground
10. Short barracks
11. Pentagonal tower
12. Long barracks
13. Commandant's house
14. Semi-circular battery

15. Officers' quarters
16. Officers' latrines
17. Storehouse
18. Hexagonal tower
19. Shops
20. Hospital
21. Scott's Space

sesquicentennial of the laying of the post's original cornerstone. The restored site celebrated the "birth of Minnesota," emphasizing the theme of national progress and anticipating the upcoming national bicentennial. With the US flag flying over the buildings, the historical interpretation focused on military pageantry, frontier heritage, and US colonization of the land. Through first-person interpretation, costumed interpreters depicted the life of the original Fifth Infantry garrison in 1827 with a focus on the history of common people. Through the 1970s and '80s the interpretive program at Historic Fort Snelling grew as buildings were reconstructed. A fur trade element was added to the program along with special events like a Memorial Day celebration and a Civil War weekend. For nearly forty years, this focus on 1827 did not produce a discussion of the concentration camp below the fort—outside the boundaries of the historic site—that most Dakota people found respectful or acceptable. And generations of Minnesotans did not learn the story.

The buildings across the river at Mendota were also preserved. Sibley moved to St. Paul in 1862, and for the rest of the nineteenth century his former home served as a school, convent, and art school. The Daughters of the American Revolution rescued the old house from ruin in 1910 and operated it for decades until turning over ownership to MNHS in 1997. The Dakota County Historical Society began providing programming at the Sibley Historic Site in 2015. The site includes not only Sibley's home but also those of traders Jean Baptiste Faribault and Hypolite Dupuis.[148]

Historic Fort Snelling became Minnesota's premier historic site. Generations of students and thousands of Minnesota residents and

Interpreters portraying regimental music at Historic Fort Snelling during the early years of the program, 1973.

FORT SNELLING AT BDOTE

tourists learned about history within its walls. World War II veterans visited Fort Snelling to remember and share their experiences. Minnesotans gathered there on Memorial Day and the Fourth of July to honor veterans and celebrate national pride. Many Minnesotans came to love Historic Fort Snelling. But for many Dakota people, the reconstructed fort represented not only the past colonization of their ancestral lands, but also the ongoing colonization of Mni Sota Makoce.

Genocide, Resilience, and Reclamation of Bdote

The Dakota survived, resisted, and kept the traditional knowledge of Mni Sota Makoce and Bdote alive in their communities after 1862. Dakota refugees began returning to Mni Sota Makoce after the war, rejoining relatives who had not left. In the two decades after the war, the number of Dakota in Minnesota fluctuated, and communities existed at Faribault, Birch Coulee, Mendota, Shakopee, Wabasha, and other places. In 1885 the federal government appropriated funds to support the Bdewakaŋtuŋwaŋ in Minnesota. It was the first payment made to the Dakota since 1861. More appropriations were made until 1899, allowing some Dakota to purchase land. By 1900, most Dakota lived in communities at Birch Coulee, Prior Lake, and Prairie Island, although many made their homes in the Twin Cities and other towns. For the next thirty years, the federal government provided virtually no support to the Minnesota Bdewakaŋtuŋwaŋ.

In 1934 the Bdewakaŋtuŋwaŋ organized under the Indian Reorganization Act. Two years later the Birch Coulee (renamed Lower Sioux) and Prairie Island communities formed with constitutions and charters. Another group of Dakota, made up of Bdewakaŋtuŋwaŋ, Sisituŋwaŋ, Waȟpetuŋwaŋ, and Iȟaŋktuŋwaŋ, organized as the Upper Sioux Community in 1938. The Shakopee Mdewakanton Sioux Community gained federal recognition in 1969 and obtained a reservation in 1972. Yet, into the twenty-first century, most Dakota continued to live outside Minnesota on reservations in Nebraska, the Dakotas, Montana, and Canada.[149]

By the late 1960s, when the American Indian Movement and other activists began to produce more Indigenous histories from Indigenous perspectives, many Americans realized that the experiences of Dakota and other Indigenous groups likely fit the definition of genocide created by the United Nations. Scholars have had various responses. Some contend that "ethnic cleansing" is a more accurate term than "genocide" because US policy focused on land acquisition, not extermination. In the 2000s some scholars started contending that the "settler colonialism" Indigenous peoples experienced in the Americas was inherently genocidal because it required colonists to eliminate Indigenous groups in order to take their land. The general consensus developing among Native people, scholars, and human rights activists is that the US government and other colonial powers committed genocide against Native Americans.[150]

In 1987, through a partnership between Dakota community members and the Minnesota Department of Natural Resources, a memorial acknowledging the history of the concentration camp at Fort Snelling was erected in Fort Snelling State Park. Dakota people founded the Dakota Memorial Relay Run in 1986 to honor their ancestors. The run begins at Fort Snelling and ends in Mankato on December 26, the day of the mass execution. Similar commemorative efforts began in the 2000s. In November 2002 a number of Dakota

Genocide

The most commonly accepted definition of genocide was established by the United Nations in 1948. The convention defined genocide as

> any of the following acts committed with intent to destroy, in whole or in part, a national, ethnical, racial or religious group, as such:
> a) Killing members of the group;
> b) Causing serious bodily or mental harm to members of the group;
> c) Deliberately inflicting on the group conditions of life calculated to bring about its physical destruction in whole or in part;
> d) Imposing measures intended to prevent births within the group;
> e) Forcibly transferring children of the group to another group.

The concentration camp at Fort Snelling was not a death camp, and Dakota people were not systematically exterminated there. The camp was, however, a part of the genocidal policies pursued against Indigenous people throughout the United States. Colonists and soldiers hunted down and killed Dakota people, abused them physically and mentally, imprisoned them, and subjected them to a campaign calculated to make them stop being Dakota. In the aftermath of the US–Dakota War, the US government separated husbands and wives for four years under grievously harsh conditions. For generations, the US government forced Dakota children to leave their families and attend boarding schools, where they were kept for years and forbidden to speak their language. And when the boarding schools were closed, the US government and welfare organizations continued to remove Dakota children from homes they judged unfit, placing them for adoption with other families.[6] ☾

people organized the Dakota Commemorative March, a walk from the Lower Sioux Reservation to Fort Snelling that has taken place in even-numbered years since then. The marches ended at the memorial in Fort Snelling State Park. In a similar tradition, beginning in 2005 Dakota people organized the Dakota 38+2 Wokiksuye Memorial Ride. Dakota people ride horses from Lower Brule, South Dakota, arriving at Mankato on December 26. They honor the thirty-eight Dakota men executed there in December 1862 as well as Śakpedaŋ and Wakaŋ Ożaŋżaŋ, who were executed at Fort Snelling in 1865.[151]

Dakota people in the Twin Cities and beyond have remained connected with Bdote sacred sites and fought to protect them. In 2005 the National Park Service (NPS) formed plans to take ownership of Mni Sni and its surrounding environment from the US Bureau of Mines. The environmental study commissioned by the NPS researched the cultural importance of the spring, concluding that Mni Sni met the criteria for a Traditional Cultural Property because of its importance to the Dakota people, both historical and ongoing. The NPS did not accept the findings of the study and noted instead that the site would remain protected as a contributing element to the Fort Snelling National Historic Landmark. Thus the spring's association with the colonizing symbol of Fort Snelling was given more importance than its status as a sacred site. This response offended many Dakota people and their allies. In 2016 the NPS manages the spring as part of a public park, and Dakota people continue to visit the spring and perform ceremonies.[152]

In 2002 developers proposed to build high-density housing on Oheyawahe, next to Acacia Cemetery. Elders representing the Dakota, Nakota, and Lakota held a pipe ceremony on the sacred site and agreed that it needed to be left alone. The elders gave the hill a new name, Wotakuye Paha, "the hill of all the relatives." Through the efforts of Dakota people, the Department of Natural Resources, the

OPPOSITE
Mni Sni, 2016.

Oheyawahe/Pilot Knob, 2016.

Trust for Public Land, Dakota County, and the Pilot Knob Preservation Association, the hill was purchased by the City of Mendota Heights. As public land, the site now features restored tallgrass prairie and bilingual Dakota/English interpretive signage describing the sacred site's importance. A limestone monument naming the seven groups of the Oceti Šakowiŋ now overlooks Bdote.[153]

In 2005 the NPS purchased the land surrounding Wakaŋ Tipi, and the area became the Bruce Vento Nature Sanctuary. The entrance to Wakaŋ Tipi is barricaded to protect it. Dakota people are part of the ongoing discussion regarding how to preserve and interpret the site. Above Wakaŋ Tipi, the ancient mounds that remain are part of Indian Mounds Park and are protected by law.

Some Dakota researchers and educators have begun teaching people about Bdote and its importance as a place. In partnership with the Minnesota Humanities Center, Allies: media/art created the Bdote Memory Map, a website available to all. The Humanities Center also regularly offers Bdote tours that stop at several sacred sites and Fort Snelling.

Historic Fort Snelling in the Twenty-First Century

For many Dakota people, Historic Fort Snelling is a symbol of colonization, colonialism, and genocide. They are critical of the reconstruction of the fort and its maintenance as a historic site by the MNHS. Some Dakota activists have argued that the interpretation of history at the historic site lacks a critical interrogation of the fort's negative role in their people's history.[154]

In May 2010 a number of Dakota activists led a "Take Down the Fort" demonstration at Historic Fort Snelling. They recounted the US–Dakota War of 1862 and the genocide perpetrated upon their people; they cited terms of Pike's "treaty" of 1805, noting the right of Dakota people to use the land under the historic fort. They argued that as a symbol of genocide and subjugation of American Indian peoples, Historic Fort Snelling should be torn down, and the land it stood upon should be returned to the Dakota. Bearing signs that read "Site of Dakota Genocide" and "Take Down the Fort, Symbol of American Imperialism," the demonstrators rallied outside the fort and then forcibly marched inside. After a peaceful protest on the parade ground, the

TAKE DOWN THE FORT

An Icon of American Imperialism

activists—threatened with arrest if they did not purchase admission—left the fort.

The demonstrators' criticisms of Historic Fort Snelling and the work of site staff members have brought changes in focus, in vocabulary, and in message to Historic Fort Snelling's programming. Similarly, leading up to the sesquicentennial of the Dred Scott decision in 2007, the NAACP and Human Rights Action of St. Paul pressed the MNHS to start telling the story of slavery and of Dred and Harriet Scott in a more prominent way. Historic Fort Snelling staff had interpreted the history of slavery over the decades, but very inconsistently. Using the external pressure as a catalyst for action, and building on previous efforts, Historic Fort Snelling staff created a space to interpret these important topics as part of the daily program.

The stories told about Fort Snelling will continue to evolve as those who care about history find more relevant and inclusive ways to tell them. Historic Fort Snelling joined the International Coalition of Sites of Conscience in 2011. The mission of the coalition is to connect the struggles of the past to present-day movements for human rights and social justice. "The need to remember often competes with the equally strong pressure to forget," notes the coalition. "Erasing the past can prevent new generations from learning critical lessons while forever compromising opportunities to build a peaceful future."[155]

On April 20, 2016, the National Trust for Historic Preservation named Historic Fort Snelling, the remaining forty-eight original buildings, and the surrounding area a national treasure: Bdote Fort Snelling. The designation is intended to help protect, sustain, and revitalize the area of the confluence and was made in consultation with Dakota people. Some Dakota people objected to the name "Bdote Fort Snelling," arguing that Bdote is *not* Fort Snelling. As discussions about the name of the confluence continued, the trust changed the name to "Fort Snelling at Bdote." Along with the MNHS, the trust envisions making the confluence a place for communities to come together.[156]

Fort Snelling at Bdote

The confluence of Mni Sota Wakpa and Ḣaḣa Wakpa, the Minnesota and Mississippi rivers, is one of the most historically significant landscapes in Minnesota. It is a place where rivers and people have come together for thousands of years. The stories of the area connect to important and difficult aspects of US history. The deeply sacred landscape of Bdote endures, telling those who pay attention of its profound significance. The buildings of Fort Snelling, both original and reconstructed, carry powerful and intermingling legacies, incorporating both the resonant stories of patriotism and sacrifice made by generations of veterans and the difficult stories of colonialism, slavery, violence, and genocide.

The stories that historians tell respond to the times in which they live, and different cultures tell different stories about their pasts. It is likely that interpretations of a place's history will conflict with each other and yet be *true* for those who tell them. With a complex and complicated past, Bdote may always be a contested space. It will certainly continue to be a place where rivers and people come together. It can also become a place where Minnesota's diverse peoples learn from each other, remember, heal, and build bridges of mutual respect.

Author's Note

Writing this book was a humbling experience. As I worked, I was continually struck by the gravity of the history that has occurred where the Mississippi and Minnesota rivers meet. I strove for sensitivity and accuracy in my word choices, and perhaps some of those choices will generate discussion as we continue to talk about this history. I have focused on the confluence as a place, which I believe fits the story both historically and currently. In all its roles—as a sacred space, a fur trade hub, a gathering place, a military post, a state park, a national historic landmark, and a national treasure—the confluence has always carried a powerful sense of place. My main goal was to provide a concise, yet holistic narrative of this place, where none had existed before. The historiography of *Fort Snelling at Bdote* is fractured (Are we talking about a fort or a confluence?) and siloed (How is World War II history connected to fur trade history?), and at times interpretations have been in direct conflict (What really happened during the US–Dakota War of 1862?). The title of this book is symbolic of its purpose: to bring stories together and remake a place in our minds to include all the histories that have occurred there. The title is also a place-name, meant to reflect that history of place and to gesture toward the placemaking that continues there. As a historian, my secondary purpose was to contextualize what has predominately been a local history within broader histories. Of these broader histories, I focused particularly on a decolonial interpretation that allowed me to interpret much of the site's history within the theoretical framework of colonialism. It seems to me that colonialism as a historical phenomenon and structure can be one of our most powerful tools for understanding what happened where the rivers come together—and what continues to happen there.

The generosity and knowledge people shared with me as I searched for answers was incredible. Many people advised me and reviewed the manuscript—too many to thank individually. My thanks to several Dakota reviewers, Historic Fort Snelling staff current and former, my colleagues at MNHS, and others who read the narrative. These advisers and reviewers, each with their own perspectives and knowledge, saved me from errors, pointed me to sources, and honed my language. Reviewers often disagreed on wording, interpretation, and facts. But these differing opinions made the text stronger and taught me important lessons. From oral tradition and memory to archaeology and history, there are many ways of knowing about the past, and we can get closest to the truth, and the meaning of it, by listening to everyone. By understanding history, we can comprehend the present and create a better future. I hope I've produced a narrative that introduces readers to the history of the confluence and provides a stepping-stone on the path toward a shared space for all.

Notes

1. Jahner, "Lakota Genesis: The Oral Tradition."

2. Westerman and White, *Mni Sota Makoce*, 18–20; Minnesota Humanities Center, "Bdote Memory Map." *Mni Sota Makoce* is an indispensable and unique resource for early Dakota history, spirituality, and information on sacred sites. I relied heavily on this text, especially in the early portions of this book, and I am indebted to the work of Westerman and White.

3. Westerman and White, *Mni Sota Makoce*, 20, 26, 92, 213; Minnesota Humanities Center, "Bdote Memory Map"; Terrell and Terrell, *Native American Context Statement*, 11, 13.

4. Westerman and White, *Mni Sota Makoce*, 186–87; Pilot Knob Preservation Association, *Oheyawahi/Pilot Knob.*

5. Arnott, Jones, and Maki, *Indian Mounds Park Mound Group*, 3–4, 19; Westerman and White, *Mni Sota Makoce*, 219.

6. Gibbon, *Archaeology of Minnesota*, ix, 38–41.

7. Gibbon, *Archaeology of Minnesota*, 40–47.

8. Gibbon, *Archaeology of Minnesota*, 13, 54–57, 59, 61; O'Connell, Jones, and Thomas, *The Minnesota Ancients*; Center for the Study of the First Americans; "Projectile Point," Collections Online, Minnesota Historical Society, http://collections.mnhs.org/cms/display.php?irn=11356653; Emerson interview.

9. Gibbon, *Archaeology of Minnesota*, 43, 66–72.

10. Gibbon, *Archaeology of Minnesota*, 74, 76–77.

11. Gibbon, *Archaeology of Minnesota*, 78–84, 88, 93.

12. Gibbon, *Archaeology of Minnesota*, 99, 144–45, 154–55; Arnott, Jones, and Maki, *Indian Mounds Park Mound Group*, 3; Bakken, *Mitakuye Owas, All My Relations*, 38–40; Birk, *The Henry Sibley Site Complex*, 4–5; Gronhovd and Andrews, *1996 and 1998 Archaeological Excavations at the Sibley House*, 92, 95; Emerson interview.

13. Gibbon, *Archaeology of Minnesota*, 159, 174; Westerman and White, *Mni Sota Makoce*, 15.

14. Minnesota Historical Society, "Tiospaye: Kinship"; Deloria, *Speaking of Indians*, 25.

15. Westerman and White, *Mni Sota Makoce*, 126; Terrell, et al., *The Cultural Meaning of Coldwater Spring*, 34–35.

16. Westerman and White, *Mni Sota Makoce*, 14; Spector, *What This Awl Means*, 11, 66–77.

17. Thwaites, ed., *The Jesuit Relations and Allied Documents*, 23:225; Akta Lakota Museum and Cultural Center, "The 'Sioux' Name and Dialects"; Gibbon, *The Sioux*, 2, 214.

18. Westerman and White, *Mni Sota Makoce*, 33–37; Perrot, "Memoir on the Manners, Customs, and Religion," 163–71.

19. Westerman and White, *Mni Sota Makoce*, 37–39.

20. Hennepin, *Description of Louisiana*, 23, 90.

21. Westerman and White, *Mni Sota Makoce*, 42.

22. Westerman and White, *Mni Sota Makoce*, 44; Goertz, "Hennepin, Louis"; Hennepin, *Description of Louisiana*, 117, 125.

23. Westerman and White, *Mni Sota Makoce*, 45.

24. Pond, "Ancient Mounds and Monuments," 144–45; Pond, *The Dakota or Sioux*, 174; Westerman and White, *Mni Sota Makoce*, 48–51; Terrell, et al., *The Cultural Meaning of Coldwater Spring*, 32.

25. Westerman and White, *Mni Sota Makoce*, 60–65, 67; Neill, "The Last French Post in the Upper Mississippi Valley," 25; Diedrich, *The Chiefs Wapahasha*, 14–19; Brik and Poseley, *The French at Lake Pepin*, 23–30.

26. For a discussion of fur trade marriages and the centrality of Native American women, see Van Kirk, *Many Tender Ties*, 4–5, 28–52.

27. Cassady, "Interpreting Kinship and Gift Giving in Dakota and Ojibwe Cultures"; Wingerd, *North Country*, 14, 40; Walker, *Lakota Religion and Belief*, 198–99.

28. Shoemaker, "A Typology of Colonialism"; Murphy, *Great Lakes Creoles*, 26.

29. Wingerd, *North Country*, 33–36; Westerman and White, *Mni Sota Makoce*, 29.

30. Westerman and White, *Mni Sota Makoce*, 72.

31. Carver, *Travels Through the Interior Parts of North America*, 63–71.

32. Carver, *Travels Through the Interior Parts of North America*, 84–91.

33. Westerman and White, *Mni Sota Makoce*, 82; Wingerd, *North Country*, 52–55.

34. Pike, *The Expeditions of Zebulon Montgomery Pike*, 44–47.

35. Pike, *The Expeditions of Zebulon Montgomery Pike*, 68–69, 74–81; Westerman and White, *Mni Sota Makoce*, 82.

36. Pike, *The Expeditions of Zebulon Montgomery Pike*, 82–84; Westerman and White, *Mni Sota Makoce*, 83; Kappler, "Treaty with the Sioux, 1805," *Indian Affairs: Laws and Treaties*.

37. Case, "Pike's Treaty"; Westerman and White, *Mni Sota Makoce*, 140–42.

38. Westerman and White, *Mni Sota Makoce*, 82, 85; Kappler, "Treaty with the Sioux of the Lakes, 1815," "Treaty with the Sioux of the St. Peter's River, 1815," and "Treaty with the Sioux, 1816," *Indian Affairs: Laws and Treaties*.

39. "Letter from the secretary of war, to the chairman of the military committee, Department of War, December 29, 1819," in Niles, ed., *Niles Weekly Register*, January 15, 1820, 330.

40. Westerman and White, *Mni Sota Makoce*, 143; Hall, *Fort Snelling*, 5, 189.

41. Westerman and White, *Mni Sota Makoce*, 143; Hall, *Fort Snelling*, 8; Sibley, *Memoir of Jean Baptiste Faribault*, 176; Forsyth, "Journal of a Voyage from St. Louis to the Falls of St. Anthony," 188–89, 200–208.

42. White, "A Dakota Invitation to Coldwater Spring"; Schoolcraft, *Narrative Journal of Travels*, 304–7; Schoolcraft, *Historical and Statistical Information*, 338, 352–53.

43. Westerman and White, *Mni Sota Makoce*, 143; Denial, "Pelagie Faribault's Island"; Deloria and DeMallie, *Documents of American Indian Diplomacy*, 1:1246.

44. Hall, *Fort Snelling*, 15–16; Shirey, "Snelling, Josiah."

45. Wingerd, *North Country*, 82–83.

46. "Historic Fort Snelling"; Hall, *Fort Snelling*, 10–11.

47. "Agriculture at Fort Snelling."

48. "Garrison Routine"; Cass, "Program Treatment Form: Married Quarters"; "Fort Snelling Commandant's House Manual."

49. Treuer, *The Assassination of Hole in the Day*, 47–49.

50. Minnesota Historical Society, Historic Fort Snelling, "The US Indian Agency (1820–1853)"; Cassady, "St. Peter's Indian Agency"; Katherine Beane, "Bde Maka Ska / Lake Calhoun, Minneapolis," in Westerman and White, *Mni Sota Makoce*, 104–7.

51. Westerman and White, *Mni Sota Makoce*, 148–55; Kappler, "Treaty With the Sauk and Foxes, etc., [July 15,] 1830," *Indian Affairs: Laws and Treaties*.

52. Bachman, *Northern Slave, Black Dakota*, 5–6, 8.

53. Bachman, *Northern Slave, Black Dakota*, 4, 8.

54. Boorom, "Interpreting African-Americans and Slavery at Fort Snelling," 3–4.

55. Bachman, *Northern Slave, Black Dakota*, 10–12; Green, *A Peculiar Imbalance*, 10–36.

56. For the story of Mariah, see the March 30, 1831, entry in "An Uncorrected Journal or Memorandum of Events &c for the Agency, Noted Daily. Indian Agency St. Peters, December 1st, 1830 and part of 1831," vol. 10, Lawrence Taliaferro Papers, Manuscript Collection, Minnesota Historical Society, St. Paul, MN; Boorom, "Interpreting African Americans and Slavery at Fort Snelling," 8; "Dred and Harriet Scott," 22–23.

57. Bachman, *Northern Slave, Black Dakota*, 20; Gilman, *Henry Hastings Sibley*, 64, 242; Henry Sibley Papers, M164, reel 17, frame 104, vol. 2, Manuscript Collection, Minnesota Historical Society, St. Paul, MN.

58. Boorom, "Interpreting African-Americans and Slavery at Fort Snelling," 6; Bachman, *Northern Slave, Black Dakota*, 15–16, 42–48.

59. Reicher, "Thompson, James"; Bachman, *Northern Slave, Black Dakota*, 11, 15–16; Wingerd, *North Country*, 236–38; Green, *A Peculiar Imbalance*, 17–36.

60. Bachman, *Northern Slave, Black Dakota*, 17, 31–32.

61. Bachman, *Northern Slave, Black Dakota*, 29–32.

62. Bachman, *Northern Slave, Black Dakota*, 33.

63. Boorom, "Interpreting African-Americans and Slavery at Fort Snelling," 9–12; Atkins, "Dred and Harriet Scott in Minnesota"; "Dred and Harriet Scott."

64. Missouri State Archives, "Missouri's Dred Scott Case."

65. Bachman, *Northern Slave, Black Dakota*, 49–51, 59–60, 64–66, 68; Seyburn, "The Tenth Regiment of Infantry."

66. Sexton, *Red River Colonist Training Manual*, 20–21; Adams, *Early Days at Red River Settlement*.

67. Gilman, *Henry Hastings Sibley*, 39, 64, 76; Minnesota Historical Society, Sibley Historic Site, "Overview"; Way, "The United States Factory System."

68. Clemmons, *Conflicted Mission*, 34–35.

69. Wingerd, *North Country*, 148.

70. Wingerd, *North Country*, 128–32.

71. Green, *A Peculiar Imbalance*, 3–4; Pengra, "Bonga, Stephen"; Kappler, "Treaty with the Chippewa, 1837," *Indian Affairs: Laws and Treaties*.

72. Wingerd, *North Country*, 132–33; "Proceedings of a Council with the Chippewa Indians," 408–32; Treuer, *The Assassination of Hole in the Day*, 63–66.

73. Wingerd, *North Country*, 133–34; Kappler, "Treaty with the Sioux, 1837," *Indian Affairs: Laws and Treaties*.

74. Wingerd, *North Country*, 135–40.

75. Wingerd, *North Country*, 155–57; Westerman and White, *Mni Sota Makoce*, 122–23; Folwell, *A History of Minnesota*, 1:422–24.

76. Wingerd, *North Country*, 139–41; Gilman, *Henry Hastings Sibley*, 79–85.

77. Wingerd, *North Country*, 148–49; Gilman, *Henry Hastings Sibley*, 76, 89; Hyde, *Empires, Nations, and Families*, 488–92; Minnesota Historical Society, Sibley Historic Site.

78. Wingerd, *North Country*, 171–73.

79. Wingerd, *North Country*, 176–79; Folwell, *A History of Minnesota*, 1:235–46.

80. Wingerd, *North Country*, 181–83.

81. Westerman and White, *Mni Sota Makoce*, 167. A stunning visual record of the Treaty of Traverse des Sioux was recorded by the artist Frank Blackwell Mayer. His sketchbooks can be viewed online at the Internet Archive (archive.org).

82. Westerman and White, *Mni Sota Makoce*, 181–82; Gilman, *Henry Hastings Sibley*, 121.

83. Snyder, ed., *The 1851 Treaty of Mendota*, 8–11.

84. Snyder, ed., *The 1851 Treaty of Mendota*, 12–13.

85. Snyder, ed., *The 1851 Treaty of Mendota*, 13–17.

86. Westerman and White, *Mni Sota Makoce*, 182–85, 188–90; White and Woolworth, *Oheyawhe or Pilot Knob*, 14–16; Snyder, *The 1851 Treaty of Mendota*, 21–23.

87. Folwell, *A History of Minnesota*, 1:278–301.

88. Wingerd, *North Country*, 196, 199.

89. Wingerd, *North Country*, 277.

90. Westerman and White, *Mni Sota Makoce*, 191–93; Prucha, ed., *Documents of United States Indian Policy*, 81; Wingerd, *North Country*, 272–78; Kappler, "Treaty with the Sioux, 1858," *Indian Affairs: Laws and Treaties*.

91. Hall, *Fort Snelling*, 25–27; Minnesota Historical Society, Sibley Historic Site, "Sibley's Political Life"; Osman, "Fort Snelling and the Civil War," 4–7.

92. Osman, *Fort Snelling and the Civil War*, 9.

93. Osman, *Fort Snelling and the Civil War*, 24–47.

94. Osman, *Fort Snelling and the Civil War*, 49–52, 186–87.

95. Osman, "General Sibley's Contraband Teamsters," 70–71; Osman, *Fort Snelling and the Civil War*, 63–67; Jackson interview.

96. Cassady and DeCarlo, "Fort Snelling in the Civil and US–Dakota Wars"; Smith, "First Minnesota Volunteer Infantry Regiment"; Carley, *Minnesota in the Civil War*, 187.

97. Anderson and Woolworth, *Through Dakota Eyes*, 8–13, 20–21, 23–27, 29–31; Carley, *The Dakota War of 1862*, 1–6; West, *Ancestry, Life, and Times of Sibley*, 263.

98. Anderson, *Little Crow*, 130–34; Anderson and Woolworth, *Through Dakota Eyes*, 13, 34–42; Carley, *The Dakota War of 1862*, 7–12.

99. From general surveys of the war to discrete studies, the estimated number of white deaths has varied widely, from just over four hundred to nearly a thousand. For a review of the literature on the deaths of white civilians, see Dahlin, *Victims of the Dakota Uprising*, 10–15. For a review of the deaths of US soldiers, see Dahlin, *Stories and Burial Places*; Anderson, "Myrick's Insult"; Anderson and Woolworth, eds., *Through Dakota Eyes*, 40–42, 56; Carley, *The Dakota War of 1862*, 15–53.

100. Stephen Osman, "Sibley's Army in November 1862," in Bakeman and Richardson, eds., *Trails of Tears*, 13, 15–17.

101. *Message of Governor Ramsey*, 12; Carley, *The Dakota War of 1862*, 59–63.

102. Board of Commissioners, *Minnesota in the Civil and Indian Wars*, 2:250, 254–55, 257; Vogel, "Rethinking the Effect of the Abrogation of the Dakota Treaties," 548. For a history of the Dakota movements into the Canadian borderlands, see McCrady, *Living with Strangers*, 17–30.

103. Osman, "Sibley's Army in November 1862," 19, 21; Monjeau-Marz, *The Dakota Indian Internment at Fort Snelling*, 53–54. For a discussion of the legality of the trials, see Bachman, *Northern Slave, Black Dakota*, Haymond, *The Infamous Dakota War Trials*, and Chomsky, "The United States–Dakota War Trials."

104. Pope to Sibley, October 7, 1862, quoted in Mary Bakeman and Alan R. Woolworth, "The Family Caravan," in Bakeman and Richardson, *Trails of Tears*, 53.

105. Bakeman and Woolworth, "The Family Caravan," 52–54; Cassady, "Why Were Dakota Non-Combatants Brought to Fort Snelling?" 4–7; Monjeau-Marz, *The Dakota Indian Internment at Fort Snelling*, 37, 40; Wilson, "Grandmother to Granddaughter"; Anderson and Woolworth, eds., *Through Dakota Eyes*, 227.

106. Monjuea-Marz, *The Dakota Indian Internment at Fort Snelling*, 38–40.

107. Bakeman and Richardson, *Trails of Tears*, 69–74; Cassady, "Why Were Dakota Non-Combatants Brought to Fort Snelling?" 5; Monjeau-Marz, *The Dakota Indian Internment at Fort Snelling*, 40–42. United States Holocaust Memorial Museum, "Concentration Camps"; email from Stephen Osman to author, May 26, 2016; Gilman, *Henry Hastings Sibley*, 189; "Petition of the chiefs and headmen of Medawakanton and Wahpakoota Sioux Indians," in *United States Congressional Serial Set*, 3569, 55th Congress, 1st Session, Senate, Report No. 4, 16–17.

108. Major General John Pope to Governor A. Ramsey, November 6, 1862, quoted in Board of Commissioners, *Minnesota in the Civil and Indian Wars*, 2:288.

109. Bachman, *Northern Slave, Black Dakota*, 285–86, 291; Anderson and Woolworth, eds., *Through Dakota Eyes*, 264; Monjeau-Marz, *The Dakota Indian Internment at Fort Snelling*, 64, 72; "Day Book, Fort Snelling, 1862–1865," vol. 45, box 16, Franklin Steele Papers, Manuscript Collection, Minnesota Historical Society, St. Paul, MN.

110. Monjeau-Marz, *The Dakota Indian Internment at Fort Snelling*, 53–59, 72–73; Anderson and Woolworth, eds., *Through Dakota Eyes*, 234, 264; Monjeau-Marz and Osman, "What You May Not Know About the Fort Snelling Indian Camps," 122–25.

111. Monjeau-Marz, *The Dakota Indian Internment at Fort Snelling*, 39, 40–41, 43, 71, 81; Millikan, "The Great Treasure of the Fort Snelling Prison Camp," 10–12; Articles of Agreement between Capt. F. M. Saunders and Franklin Steele, January 1, 1863, Franklin Steele Papers, box 7, folder "Correspondence and Business Papers, Jan–May 15, 1863," Manuscript Collection, Minnesota Historical Society, St. Paul, MN.

112. Carley, *The Dakota War of 1862*, 70–75.

113. Bachman, *Northern Slave, Black Dakota*, 262–63; Vogel, "Rethinking the Effect of the Abrogation of the Dakota Treaties"; Treuer, *The Assassination of Hole in the Day*, 130–44.

114. Monjeau-Marz, *The Dakota Indian Internment at Fort Snelling*, 99–100, 107–8; Lass, "The Removal from Minnesota of the Sioux and Winnebago Indians," 360–63; Gilman, *Henry Hastings Sibley*, 191. For an overview of the Dakota and Ho-Chunk experience at Crow Creek, see Hyman, "Survival at Crow Creek."

115. Osman, "General Sibley's Contraband Teamsters," 60–63; Wilson, "Hickman, Robert T."; Monjeau-Marz, *The Dakota Indian Internment at Fort Snelling*, 107; Green, *A Peculiar Imbalance*, 127–39; WPA Writer's Project, Slave Narratives, "Hickman, Rev. Robert Hickman"; Taylor, "Pilgrim's Progress," 24–26; Spangler, *The Negro in Minnesota*, 51–54.

116. Wingerd, *North Country*, 329–30; Minnesota Historical Society, "Bounties."

117. Osman, "General Sibley's Contraband Teamsters," 65. The most comprehensive history of the Punitive Expeditions is Beck, *Columns of Vengeance*; see also Bergemann, *Brackett's Battalion*.

118. Monjeau-Marz, *The Dakota Indian Internment at Fort Snelling*, 122–23; Osman, "General Sibley's Contraband Teamsters," 70–71.

119. Monjeau-Marz, *The Dakota Indian Internment at Fort Snelling*, 111–21; Minnesota Historical Society, Historic Fort Snelling, "The US–Dakota War of 1862"; Osman, *Fort Snelling and the Civil War*, 167–73; DeCarlo, "Borderland to Bordered Land."

120. Carlson, "They Tell Their Story," 265.

121. Hall, *Fort Snelling*, 29.

122. Steward, *Buffalo Soldiers*, 86–91; Schubert, *Voices of the Buffalo Soldier*, 47–50.

123. Nankivell, *Buffalo Soldier Regiment*, 37–41.

124. Holbrook, *Minnesota in the Spanish-American War*, 11, 109, 112–14.

125. Roise and Peterson, *Fort Snelling's Buildings 17, 18, 22, and 30*.

126. Roise and Peterson, *Fort Snelling's Buildings 17, 18, 22, and 30*, 110–11; For a narrative of the Battle of Sugar Point, see Mattsen, "The Battle of Sugar Point."

127. Holbrook and Appel, *Minnesota in the War with Germany*, 137, 139, 174, 177, 188; Minnesota Historical Society, Historic Fort Snelling, "The Fort Expands."

128. For a history of General Hospital 29, see *Reveille, The Call to a New Life.*

129. *Book of Champions, Summer Sports*; Slovak, "Smartest Horse in the U.S. Army."

130. *Citizens Military Training Camp*; *Handbook Camp Snelling*; *Round Tower*, 1923 and 1925; *Military Show, Fort Snelling.*

131. Hall, *Fort Snelling*, 32; Osman, *Fort Snelling Then and Now*, 37.

132. US Army Memorial Affairs Agency, *Fort Snelling National Cemetery*; Chicoine, *Our Hallowed Ground*, xviii.

133. Osman, *Fort Snelling Then and Now*, 8, 11–14.

134. Holmquist, ed., *They Chose Minnesota*, 558; "Bud Nakasone—What Fort Snelling Means to Me," https://www.youtube.com/watch?v=VdGf82utrIA.

135. DeCarlo, "Military Intelligence Service Language School."

136. Hall, *Fort Snelling*, 32.

137. Chicoine, *Our Hallowed Ground*; Minnesota Historical Society, Fort Snelling, "Fort Snelling National Cemetery"; US Department of Veterans Affairs, National Cemetery Administration, "Fort Snelling National Cemetery."

138. O'Brien, et al., *The Cultural Meaning of Coldwater Spring*, 20.

139. Anfinson, "Spiritual Power to Industrial Might," 256, 260, 262, 264–66; Minnesota Historical Society, Mill City Museum, "Minneapolis Flour Milling Boom"; Ryder, "Phantom of the River," 17–21; Lurie, "A History of Owamni Yomni."

140. Nelson, "Indian Mounds Park."

141. Woolworth and Woolworth, "Carver: Little Cave, Big History."

142. Westerman and White, *Mni Sota Makoce*, 186–87.

143. "Round Tower Dedicated as Shrine, Museum, Monument," *Minneapolis Star Journal*, June 15, 1940.

144. Thomas H. Swain, Executive Director MHS to W. D. Aesechbacher, Secretary Treasurer, Mississippi Valley Historical Association, June 12, 1958, Minnesota Statehood Centennial Commission Files, 1957–58, box 2, folder "Fort Snelling—Restoration," Manuscript Collection, Minnesota Historical Society, St. Paul, MN.

145. Thomas H. Swain to Charles T. Burnley, November 8, 1957, and Russel W. Fridley to MHS Members, December 12, 1957, Minnesota Statehood Centennial Commission Files, 1957–58, box 2, Manuscript Collection, Minnesota Historical Society, St. Paul, MN; John Callender, "Restoration of Fort Snelling: Progress Report—Project 07," May 27, 1958, and John Callender, "A Report to the Commission; Archaeological Exploration of Old Fort Snelling," Fall 1957, both Minnesota Statehood Centennial Commission Files, 1957–58, box 2, folder "Fort Snelling—Restoration," Manuscript Collection, Minnesota Historical Society, St. Paul, MN; Bodnar, *Remaking America*, 154–58.

146. Fort Snelling Sesquicentennial Committee, *Fort Snelling Sesquicentennial Committee Report.*

147. Minnesota Historical Society, Historic Fort Snelling, "Archaeology and the Restoration of Historic Fort Snelling."

148. Friends of the Sibley Historic Site, "Houses of the Sibley Historic Site"; Minnesota Historical Society, Sibley Historic Site.

149. Westerman and White, *Mni Sota Makoce*, 203, 207; Hyman, *Dakota Women's Work*, 8–9; Shakopee Mdewakanton Sioux Community, "Our History"; Prairie Island Indian Community, "Community"; Lower Sioux Indian Community, "About Us"; Upper Sioux Community, "History"; State of Minnesota, Indian Affairs Council, "Overview of Indian Tribes in Minnesota."

150. Dunbar-Ortiz, *An Indigenous Peoples' History of the United States*, 6–10.

151. Waziyatawin Angela Wilson, "Manipi Hena Owas'in Wicunkiksuyapi (We Remember All Those Who Walked)," in Wilson, ed., *In the Footsteps of Our Ancestors*, 1; Hagerty, *Dakota 38*; Friends of Fort Snelling, Fort Snelling State Park Association, "Creating Fort Snelling State Park"; Niskanen and Ohman, *Prairie, Lake, Forest*, 152–54.

152. Westerman and White, *Mni Sota Makoce*, 215–16; National Park Service, Mississippi River & Recreation Area, "Coldwater Spring"; Pilot Knob/Oheyawahi Preservation Association.

153. Trust for Public Land, "Pilot Knob Bluff Protected."

154. Waziyatawin, *What Does Justice Look Like?*, 101.

155. International Coalition of Sites of Conscience, quote from "About Us."

156. National Trust for Historic Preservation, "Bdote Fort Snelling."

Notes to Sidebars

1. Westerman and White, *Mni Sota Makoce*, 22; Minnesota Historical Society, "Oceti Śakowiŋ— The Seven Council Fires"; Sprecher, *Oceti Śakowiŋ*.

2. For an analysis of the Doctrine of Discovery, see Miller, et al., *Discovering Indigenous Lands*, Stannard, *American Holocaust*, 65; Dörr, "The Background of the Theory of Discovery."

3. For works that analyze the United States as an empire, see Immerwahr, *How to Hide an Empire* and Saler, *The Settler's Empire*.

4. Madley, *An American Genocide*, 15; Dunbar-Ortiz, *An Indigenous Peoples' History of the United States*, 6–10; Cavanagh and Veracini, "Definition"; LeFevre, "Settler Colonialism." For theoretical works on settler colonialism, see Wolfe, *Settler Colonialism and the Transformation of Anthropology*, Veracini, *Settler Colonialism*, and Hixson, *American Settler Colonialism*. For the relationship between settler colonialism and genocide, see Moses, ed., *Empire, Colony, Genocide*.

5. United States Holocaust Memorial Museum, "Concentration Camps"; *Oxford English Dictionary*, "Internment Camp." For a discussion of Indigenous sovereignty in 1862, see Haymond, *The Infamous Dakota War Trials*, 65–68.

6. Waziyatawin, *What Does Justice Look Like?*, 37–62; United Nations, *Convention on the Prevention and Punishment of the Crime of Genocide*.

Bibliography

Adams, Ann. *Early Days at Red River Settlement, and Fort Snelling.* St. Paul: Minnesota Historical Society, 1894.

"Agriculture at Fort Snelling." Historic Fort Snelling Training Materials, n.d.

Akta Lakota Museum and Cultural Center. "The 'Sioux' Name and Dialects." http://aktalakota .stjo.org/site/PageServer?pagename=alm _culture_origins.

Anderson, Gary Clayton. *Ethnic Cleansing and the Indian: The Crime That Should Haunt America.* Norman: University of Oklahoma Press, 2014.

———. *Little Crow: Spokesman for the Sioux.* St. Paul: Minnesota Historical Society Press, 1986.

———. "Myrick's Insult: A Fresh Look at Myth and Reality." *Minnesota History* 48, no. 5 (Spring 1983): 198–206.

Anderson, Gary Clayton, and Alan R. Woolworth, eds. *Through Dakota Eyes: Narrative Accounts of the Minnesota Indian War of 1862.* St. Paul: Minnesota Historical Society Press, 1988.

Anfinson, John O. "Spiritual Power to Industrial Might: 12,000 Years at St. Anthony Falls." *Minnesota History* 58, no. 5/6 (Spring/Summer 2003): 252–69.

Arnott, Sigrid, Geoff Jones, and David Maki. *Indian Mounds Park Mound Group National Register of Historic Places Registration Form.* Minneapolis, MN: Archaeo-Physics LLC, 2013.

Atkins, Annette. "Dred and Harriet Scott in Minnesota." MNopedia, October 13, 2014.

Bachman, Walt. *Northern Slave, Black Dakota: The Life and Times of Joseph Godfrey.* Bloomington, MN: Pond Dakota Press, 2013.

Bakeman, Mary H., and Antona M. Richardson, eds. *Trails of Tears: Minnesota's Dakota Indian Exile Begins.* Roseville, MN: Prairie Echoes Press, Park Genealogical Books, 2008.

Bakken, Kent, et al. *Mitakuye Owas, All My Relations: Authentication, Recovery and Reburial at the Lincoln Mounds for the Bloomington Central Station Project, Bloomington, Minnesota.* 2006.

Beck, Paul N. *Columns of Vengeance: Soldiers, Sioux, and the Punitive Expeditions 1863–1864.* Norman: University of Oklahoma Press, 2013.

Bergemann, Kurt D. *Brackett's Battalion: Minnesota Cavalry in the Civil War and Dakota War.* St. Paul: Minnesota Historical Society Press, 2004.

Birk, Douglas A. *The Henry Sibley Site Complex (21DK31) Brick House Archaeological Project: Exterior East Wall Investigations.* Minneapolis: Institute of Minnesota Archaeology, 1993.

Birk, Douglas A., and Judy Poseley. *The French at Lake Pepin: An Archaeological Survey For Fort Beauharnois.* St. Paul: Minnesota Historical Society, 1978.

Board of Commissioners. *Minnesota in the Civil and Indian Wars, 1861–1865.* 2 vols. St. Paul, MN: Pioneer Press Company, 1893.

Bodnar, John. *Remaking America: Public Memory, Commemoration, and Patriotism in the Twentieth Century.* Princeton, NJ: Princeton University Press, 1992.

Book of Champions, Summer Sports—Forty Ninth Infantry: Fort Snelling, Minnesota, Season 1921. [Fort Snelling, MN: n.p., 1921?].

Boorom, Jeff. "Interpreting African-Americans and Slavery at Fort Snelling." Fort Snelling Training Materials, May 2007.

Carley, Kenneth. *The Dakota War of 1862: Minnesota's Other Civil War.* St. Paul: Minnesota Historical Society Press, 1976.

———. *Minnesota in the Civil War: An Illustrated History.* St. Paul: Minnesota Historical Society Press, 2000.

Carlson, Sarah-Eva Ellen. "They Tell Their Story: The Dakota Internment at Camp McClellan in Davenport, 1862–1866." *The Annals of Iowa* 63, no. 3 (Summer 2004): 251–78.

Carver, Jonathan. *Travels Through the Interior Parts of North America.* London: J. Phillips, 1781.

Case, Martin W. "'Pike's Treaty'—One Bdote Area Myth." Bdote Memory Map, March 14, 2010. https://bdote.wordpress.com/2010/03/14/pike-treaty-the-bdote-area-myth/.

Cass, Nancy. "Program Treatment Form: Married Quarters." Fort Snelling Training Materials, 2013.

Cassady, Matthew. "Interpreting Kinship and Gift Giving in Dakota and Ojibwe Cultures." Historic Fort Snelling Training Materials, 2015.

———. "St. Peter's Indian Agency—Daily Base Program SOP." Fort Snelling Training Materials, March 8, 2011.

———. "Why Were Dakota Non-Combatants Brought to Fort Snelling After the US-Dakota War of 1862?" Typescript, 2012.

Cassady, Matthew, and Peter J. DeCarlo. "Fort

Snelling in the Civil and US–Dakota Wars, 1861–1866." MNopedia, November 23, 2015.

Cavanagh, Edward, and Lorenzo Veracini. "Definition." SettlerColonialStudies.org (blog).

Chicoine, Stephen. *Our Hallowed Ground: World War II Veterans of Fort Snelling National Cemetery.* Minneapolis: University of Minnesota Press, 2005.

Chomsky, Carol. "The United States–Dakota War Trials: A Study in Military Injustice." *Stanford Law Review* 43 (1990): 13.

Citizens Military Training Camp, Red Course, Fort Snelling, Minnesota, 1921. [MN: n.p., 1921?].

Clemmons, Linda M. *Conflicted Mission: Faith, Disputes, and Deception on the Dakota Frontier.* St. Paul: Minnesota Historical Society Press, 2014.

Colwell-Chanthaphonh, C., and T. J. Ferguson. "Intersecting Magisteria: Bridging Archaeological Science and Traditional Knowledge." *Journal of Social Archaeology* 10, no. 3 (2010): 325–46.

Dahlin, Curtis A. *The Stories and Burial Places of Civil War Soldiers and Militia Killed in Battles with the Dakota.* Roseville, MN: The author, 2013.

———. *Victims of the Dakota Uprising: Killed, Wounded and Captured.* Roseville, MN: The author, 2012.

DeCarlo, Peter. "Military Intelligence Service Language School (MISLS)." MNopedia, May 13, 2015.

DeCarlo, Peter J. "Borderland to Bordered Land: Colonial Struggles Between the Bdewákhaŋthuŋwaŋ Dakhóta, the US Army, and the Hudson's Bay Company at the Forty-Ninth Parallel, 1863–1865." *The Northern Midwest and the US–Canadian Borderlands: Essays on a Lost Region,* edited by Jon K. Lauck and Gleaves Whitney, East Lansing: Michigan State University Press, 2020.

Deloria, Ella. *Speaking of Indians.* New York: Friendship Press, 1944. Reprint, Lincoln: University of Nebraska Press, 1998.

Deloria, Vine Jr., and Raymond J. DeMallie. *Documents of American Indian Diplomacy: Treaties, Agreements, and Conventions, 1775–1979.* Vol. 1. Norman: University of Oklahoma Press, 1999.

Denial, Catherine J. *Making Marriage: Husbands, Wives and the American State in Dakota and Ojibwe Country.* St. Paul: Minnesota Historical Society Press, 2013.

———. "Pelagie Faribault's Island: Property, Kinship, and the Meaning of Marriage in Dakota Country." *Minnesota History* 62, no. 2 (Summer 2010): 48–59.

Diedrich, Mark. *The Chiefs Wapahasha: Three Generations of Dakota Leadership, 1740–1876.* Rochester, MN: Coyote Books, 2004.

Dörr, Dieter. "The Background of the Theory of Discovery." *American Indian Law Review* 38, no. 2 (2013–14): 477–99.

"Dred and Harriet Scott: Slavery Interpretive Manual." Fort Snelling Training Materials, 2012.

Dunbar-Ortiz, Roxanne. *An Indigenous Peoples' History of the United States.* Boston, MA: Beacon Press, 2014.

Emerson, Patricia, Director, Archaeology Department, Minnesota Historical Society, conversation, April 13, 2016.

Feshir, Riham. "Historic Fort Snelling Named 'National Treasure,'" MPR News, April 20, 2016.

Folwell, William Watts. *A History of Minnesota.* Vol. 1. St. Paul: Minnesota Historical Society Press, 1956.

Forsyth, Thomas. "Journal of a Voyage from St. Louis to the Falls of St. Anthony, in 1819." *Collections of the State Historical Society of Wisconsin* 6 (1908): 188–219.

"Fort Snelling Commandant's House Manual." Historic Fort Snelling Training Materials, 2016.

Fort Snelling Sesquicentennial Committee. *Fort Snelling Sesquicentennial Committee Report.* St. Paul, MN: The Committee, 1969.

Friends of Fort Snelling, Fort Snelling State Park Association. "Creating Fort Snelling State Park."

Friends of the Sibley Historic Site. "Houses of the Sibley Historic Site." http://www.sibley-friends.org/sibleyhouse.htm.

"Garrison Routine." Historic Fort Snelling Training Materials, 2010.

Gibbon, Guy. *Archaeology of Minnesota: The Prehistory of the Upper Mississippi River Region.* Minneapolis: University of Minnesota Press, 2012.

———. *The Sioux: The Dakota and Lakota Nations.* Malden, MA: Blackwell Publishing, 2003.

Gilman, Carolyn. *Where Two Worlds Meet: The Great Lakes Fur Trade.* St. Paul: Minnesota Historical Society Press, 1982.

Gilman, Rhoda R. *Henry Hastings Sibley: Divided Heart.* St. Paul: Minnesota Historical Society Press, 2004.

Goetz, Kathryn R. "Hennepin, Louis (ca. 1640–ca. 1701)." MNopedia, August 12, 2013.

Green, William D. *A Peculiar Imbalance: The Fall and Rise of Racial Equality in Early Minnesota.* St. Paul: Minnesota Historical Society Press, 2007.

Gronhovd, Amanda, Grant Day, and Susan Andrews. *1996 and 1998 Archaeological Excavations at the Sibley House.*

Hagerty, Silas. *Dakota 38.* Portland, ME: Smooth Feather Productions, 2012. http://smooth feather.com/dakota38/?page_id=7.

Hall, Steve. *Fort Snelling: Colossus of the Wilderness.* St. Paul: Minnesota Historical Society Press, 1987.

Handbook Camp Snelling. 1927. [MN: Fort Snelling, 1927].

Haymond, John A. *The Infamous Dakota War Trials of 1862: Revenge, Military Law and the Judgment of History.* Jefferson, NC: McFarland and Company, Inc., 2016.

Hennepin, Louis. *Description of Louisiana.* Translated by Marion E. Cross. Minneapolis: University of Minnesota Press, 1980.

"Historic Fort Snelling." Typescript. Historic Fort Snelling Training Materials, n.d.

Hixson, Walter L. *American Settler Colonialism: A History.* New York: Palgrave Macmillan, 2013.

Holbrook, Franklin F. *Minnesota in the Spanish-American War and Philippine Insurrection.* St. Paul: Minnesota War Records Commission, 1923.

Holbrook, Franklin F., and Livia Appel. *Minnesota in the War with Germany.* St. Paul: Minnesota Historical Society, 1928–32.

Holmquist, June Drenning, ed. *They Chose Minnesota: A Survey of the State's Ethnic Groups.* St. Paul: Minnesota Historical Society Press, 1981.

Hyde, Anne F. *Empires, Nations, and Families: A New History of the North American West, 1800–1860.* Lincoln: University of Nebraska Press, 2011.

Hyman, Colette A. *Dakota Women's Work: Creativity, Culture, and Exile.* St. Paul: Minnesota Historical Society Press, 2012.

———. "Survival at Crow Creek, 1863–1866." *Minnesota History* 61, no. 4 (Winter 2008-09): 148–61.

Immerwahr, Daniel. *How to Hide an Empire: A History of the Greater United States.* New York: Farrar, Straus, and Giroux, 2019.

International Coalition of Sites of Conscience. http://www.sitesofconscience.org/.

Jackson, Franky, interview, May 20, 2018.

Jahner, Elaine A. "Lakota Genesis: The Oral Tradition." In *Sioux Indian Religion: Tradition and Innovation,* edited by Raymond J. DeMallie and Douglas R. Parks, 45–65. Norman: University of Oklahoma Press, 1987.

Kappler, Charles J. *Indian Affairs: Laws and Treaties.* Vol. 2. Washington, DC: Government Printing Office, 1904. Oklahoma State University Library has built a searchable online resource of all the treaties in this volume: https://dc.library.okstate.edu/digital/collection/kapplers.

Lass, William E. "The Removal from Minnesota of the Sioux and Winnebago Indians." *Minnesota History* 38, no. 8 (1963): 360–64.

LeFevre, Tate A. "Settler Colonialism." Oxford Bibliographies (online), May 29, 2015.

Lower Sioux Indian Community. "About Us." http://lowersioux.com/about-us/.

Lurie, Jon. "A History of Owamni Yomni: Lock Closures Signal Healing for Mississippi River." *The Circle (Minneapolis),* July 19, 2015.

Madley, Benjamin. *An American Genocide: The United States and the California Indian Catastrophe.* New Haven, CT: Yale University Press, 2016.

Mattsen, William E. "The Battle of Sugar Point: A Reexamination." *Minnesota History* 50, no. 7 (Fall 1987): 269–75.

McCrady, David G. *Living with Strangers: The Nineteenth-Century Sioux and the Canadian-American Borderlands.* Toronto: University of Toronto Press, 2006.

Message of Governor Ramsey to the Legislature of Minnesota, Delivered September 9, 1862. St. Paul, MN: WM. R. Marshall, State Printer, 1862.

Military Show, Fort Snelling, September 28 29 30 1928: Program and Exhibits Guide.

Miller, Robert J., et al. *Discovering Indigenous Lands: The Doctrine of Discovery in the English Colonies.* New York: Oxford University Press, 2010.

Millikan, William. "The Great Treasure of the Fort Snelling Prison Camp." *Minnesota History* 62, no. 1 (Spring 2010): 4–17.

Minnesota Historical Society. "Bounties." The US–Dakota War of 1862. http://www.usdakotawar.org/history/aftermath/bounties.

———. "Oceti Šakowiŋ—The Seven Council Fires." http://mnhs.org/sevencouncilfires.

———. "Tiošpaye: Kinship." The US–Dakota War of 1862. http://www.usdakotawar.org/history/dakota-homeland-oceti-šakowiŋ/tiošpaye-kinship.

Minnesota Historical Society, Historic Fort Snelling. http://www.historicfortsnelling.org/.

———. "Archaeology and the Restoration of Historic Fort Snelling." http://www.mnhs.org/fortsnelling/learn/archaeology.

———. "The Fort Expands." https://www.mnhs.org/fortsnelling/learn/military-history/fort-expands.

———. "Fort Snelling National Cemetery." http://www.mnhs.org/fortsnelling/learn/military-history/national-cemetery.

———. "The US–Dakota War of 1862." http://www.mnhs.org/fortsnelling/learn/us-dakota-war.

———. "The US Indian Agency (1820–1853)." http://www.mnhs.org/fortsnelling/learn/native-americans/us-indian-agency.

Minnesota Historical Society, Mill City Museum. "Minneapolis Flour Milling Boom." http://www.mnhs.org/millcity/learn/history/flour-milling.

Minnesota Historical Society, Sibley Historic Site. http://sites.mnhs.org/historic-sites/sibley-historic-site.

———. "Overview." http://www.mnhs.org/sibley/learn.

———."Sibley's Political Life." http://www.mnhs.org/sibley/learn/henry-hastings-sibley.

Minnesota Humanities Center. "Bdote Memory Map." http://bdotememorymap.org/.

Minnesota Statehood Centennial Commission. Administrative Files. Manuscript Collection, Minnesota Historical Society, St. Paul.

Missouri State Archives. "Missouri's Dred Scott Case, 1846–1857." Missouri Digital Heritage. https://www.sos.mo.gov/archives/resources/africanamerican/scott/scott.asp.

Monjeau-Marz, Corinne L. The Dakota Indian Internment at Fort Snelling, 1862–1864. St. Paul, MN: Prairie Smoke Press, 2006.

Monjeau-Marz, Corinne L., and Stephen Osman. "What You May Not Know About the Fort Snelling Indian Camps." Minnesota's Heritage 7 (January 2013): 112–33.

Moses, A. Dirk, ed. Empire, Colony, Genocide: Conquest, Occupation, and Subaltern Resistance in World History. New York: Berghahn Books, 2008.

Murphy, Lucy Eldersveld. Great Lakes Creoles: A French-Indian Community on the Northern Borderlands, Prairie Du Chien, 1750–1860. New York: Cambridge University Press, 2014.

Nankivell, John H. Buffalo Soldier Regiment: History of the Twenty-fifth United States Infantry, 1869–1926. Lincoln: University of Nebraska Press, 2001.

National Park Service, Mississippi River and Recreation Area. "Coldwater Spring." https://www.nps.gov/miss/planyourvisit/coldwater.htm.

National Trust for Historic Preservation. "Bdote Fort Snelling." http://savingplaces.org/places/bdote-fort-snelling.

Neill, E. D. "The Last French Post in the Upper Mississippi Valley." Magazine of Western History 7, no. 1 (November 1887): 17–29.

Nelson, Paul. "Indian Mounds Park, St. Paul." MNopedia, July 27, 2016.

Niles, Hezekiah, ed. Niles' Weekly Register. Vol. 17. Baltimore, MD: Franklin Press, 1820.

Niskanen, Chris, and Doug Ohman. Prairie, Lake, Forest: Minnesota's State Parks. St. Paul: Minnesota Historical Society Press, 2010.

O'Brien, Mollie M., et al. The Cultural Meaning of Coldwater Spring: Final Ethnographic Resources Study of the Former US Bureau of Mines Twin Cities Research Center Property, Hennepin County, Minnesota. St. Paul, MN: Summit Envirosolutions Inc., 2006.

O'Connell, Barbara, James L. Jones, and Bruce Thomas. The Minnesota Ancients: Browns Valley and Pelican Rapids. [MN]: n.p., n.d.

Osman, Stephen E. Fort Snelling and the Civil War. St. Paul, MN: Ramsey County Historical Society, 2017.

———. Fort Snelling Then and Now: The World War II Years. St. Paul, MN: Friends of Fort Snelling, 2011.

———. "General Sibley's Contraband Teamsters." Minnesota's Heritage 7 (January 2013): 54–74.

Oxford English Dictionary. "Internment Camp."

Pengra, Lilah Morton. "Bonga, Stephen (1799–1884)." Blackpast.org. http://www.blackpast.org/aah/bonga-stephen-1799-1884.

Perrot, Nicolas. "Memoir on the Manners, Customs, and Religion of the Savages of North America." The Indian Tribes of the Upper Mississippi Valley and Region of the Great Lakes. Edited and translated by Emma Helen Blair. Lincoln: University of Nebraska Press, 1996.

Pike, Zebulon Montgomery. The Expeditions of Zebulon Montgomery Pike. Edited by Elliot Coues. New York: Francis Harper, 1895.

Pilot Knob Preservation Association. Oheyawahi/Pilot Knob Mendota Heights Minnesota. [MN:

n.p., 2010]. http://www.pilotknobpreservation
.org/47849%20Pilot%20Knob%20Guide%20
new%20web%20version.pdf.

Pilot Knob/Oheyawahi Preservation Association.
http://pilotknobpreservation.org.

Pond, Gideon. "Ancient Mounds and Monuments."
Minnesota Historical Society Collections 1 (1915–
16): 144–52.

Pond, Samuel W. *The Dakota or Sioux in Minnesota
as They Were in 1834.* 1908. Reprint, St. Paul:
Minnesota Historical Society Press, 1986.

Prairie Island Indian Community. "Community."
http://prairieisland.org/community/.

"Proceedings of a Council with the Chippewa Indians." *Iowa Journal of History and Politics* 9 (1911):
433–37.

Prucha, Francis Paul, ed. *Documents of United States
Indian Policy.* 3rd edition. Lincoln: University of
Nebraska Press, 2000.

Reicher, Matt. "Thompson, James (c.1799–1884)."
MNopedia, May 12, 2014.

*Reveille, The Call to a New Life: Centennial Memo-
rial of Fort Snelling.* Fort Snelling, MN: US General Hospital 29, 1919.

Roise, Charlene, and Penny Peterson. *Fort Snelling's
Buildings 17, 18, 22, and 30: Their Evolution and
Context.* Minneapolis, MN: Hess, Roise and Co.,
2008.

Round Tower [periodical], 1923 and 1925.

Ryder, Franklin J. "Phantom of the River: Spirit
Island's Life and Death." *Hennepin History* 31,
no. 2 (Spring 1972): 16–21.

Saler, Bethel. *The Settler's Empire: Colonialism and
State Formation in America's Old Northwest.*
Philadelphia: University of Pennsylvania Press,
2015.

Schoolcraft, Henry. *Historical and Statistical Information Respecting the History, Condition and
Prospects of the Indian Tribes of the United States.*
Philadelphia, PA: Lippincott, Grambo and Co.,
1851.

———. *Narrative Journal of Travels.* Albany, NY: E.
and E. Hosford, 1821.

Schubert, Frank N. *Voices of the Buffalo Soldier:
Records, Reports, and Recollections of Military
Life and Service in the West.* Albuquerque: Uni-
versity of New Mexico Press, 2003.

Seyburn, Lt. S. Y. "The Tenth Regiment of Infantry."
Center of Military History, November 12, 2015.
http://www.history.army.mil/books/r&h/R&H-
10IN.htm.

Sexton, Mary Ann. *Red River Colonist Training
Manual.* St. Paul: Minnesota Historical Society,
1991.

Shakopee Mdewakanton Sioux Community. "Our
History." https://shakopeedakota.org/culture
/our-native-american-history.

Shaw, Thomas. "'1820s Sketch of New Hope' Discovered by Thomas Shaw." *Friends of Fort Snelling*
(December 2007).

Shirey, Sarah. "Snelling, Josiah (1782–1828)."
MNopedia, January 6, 2016.

Shoemaker, Nancy. "A Typology of Colonialism."
Perspectives on History (October 2015).

Sibley, H. H. *Memoir of Jean Baptiste Faribault.* St.
Paul: Minnesota Historical Society, 1880.

Sibley, Henry H. Papers. Manuscript Collection,
Minnesota Historical Society, St. Paul.

Slovak, Marilyn L. "'Smartest Horse in the U.S.
Army': Whiskey of Fort Snelling." *Minnesota
History* 61 (Winter 2009–10): 336–45.

Smith, Hampton. "First Minnesota Volunteer
Infantry Regiment." MNopedia, March 13, 2012.

Snyder, Rebecca, ed. *The 1851 Treaty of Mendota.*
South St. Paul, MN: Dakota County Historical
Society, 2002.

Spangler, Earl. *The Negro in Minnesota.* Minneapolis, MN: T. S. Denison, 1961.

Spector, Janet. *What This Awl Means: Feminist
Archaeology at a Wahpeton Dakota Village.* St.
Paul: Minnesota Historical Society Press, 1993.

Sprecher, James P. *Oceti Sakowin—The People of the
Seven Council Fires.* Vermillion: South Dakota
Public Broadcasting, 2007. http://watch.sdpb.
org/video/1472853204.

Stannard, David E. *American Holocaust: The Conquest of the New World.* New York: Oxford University Press, 1992.

State of Minnesota, Indian Affairs Council. "Overview of Indian Tribes in Minnesota."

Steele, Franklin. Papers. Manuscript Collection,
Minnesota Historical Society, St. Paul.

Steward, T. G. *Buffalo Soldiers: The Colored Regu-
lars in the United States Army.* Philadelphia, PA:
A.M.E. Book Concern, 1904.

Taliaferro, Lawrence. Papers. Manuscript Collection, Minnesota Historical Society, St. Paul.

Taylor, David Vassar. "Pilgrim's Progress: Black St.
Paul and the Making of an Urban Ghetto, 1870–
1939." PhD diss., University of Minnesota, 1977.

Terrell, Eva B., and Michelle M. Terrell. *Native American Context Statement and Reconnaissance*

Level Survey Supplement. Shafer, MN: Two Pines Resource Group, 2016.

Terrell, Michelle M., et al. *The Cultural Meaning of Coldwater Spring: Final Ethnographic Resources Study of the Former U.S. Bureau of Mines Twin Cities Research Center Property, Hennepin County, Minnesota.* St. Paul, MN: Summit Envirosolutions, Inc., 2006.

Thwaites, Reuben Gold, ed. *The Jesuit Relations and Allied Documents.* 73 vol. Cleveland, OH: Burrows Brothers Company, 1928.

Treuer, Anton. *The Assassination of Hole in the Day.* St. Paul: Minnesota Historical Society Press, 2011.

Trust for Public Land. "Pilot Knob Bluff Protected (MN)." December 22, 2005. https://www.tpl.org/media-room/pilot-knob-bluff-protected-mn.

United Nations. *Convention on the Prevention and Punishment of the Crime of Genocide. Adopted by the General Assembly of the United Nations on 9 December 1948.*

US Army Memorial Affairs Agency. *Fort Snelling National Cemetery.* Washington, DC: Government Printing Office, 1972.

US Department of Veterans Affairs, National Cemetery Administration. "Fort Snelling National Cemetery." http://www.cem.va.gov/CEMs/nchp/ftsnelling.asp.

United States Holocaust Memorial Museum. "Concentration Camps, 1933–1939." https://encyclopedia.ushmm.org/content/en/article/concentration-camps-1933-39.

Upper Sioux Community. "History." http://www.uppersiouxcommunity-nsn.gov/page/history.

Van Kirk, Sylvia. *Many Tender Ties: Women in Fur Trade Society, 1670–1870.* Norman: University of Oklahoma Press, 1980.

Veracini, Lorenzo. *Settler Colonialism: A Theoretical Overview.* New York: Palgrave Macmillan, 2010.

Vogel, Howard J. "Rethinking the Effect of the Abrogation of the Dakota Treaties and the Authority for the Removal of the Dakota People from Their Homeland." *William Mitchell Law Review* 39, no. 2 (2013): 538–81.

Walker, James R. *Lakota Religion and Belief.* Lincoln: University of Nebraska Press, 1980.

Warren, William W. *History of the Ojibwe People.* St. Paul: Minnesota Historical Society Press, 1984.

Way, Royal B. "The United States Factory System for Trading with the Indians, 1796–1822." *Mississippi Valley Historical Review* 6, no. 2 (September 1919): 220–35.

Waziyatawin. *What Does Justice Look Like? The Struggle for Liberation in Dakota Homeland.* St. Paul, MN: Living Justice Press, 2008.

West, Nathaniel. *The Ancestry, Life, and Times of Hon. Henry Hastings Sibley.* St. Paul, MN: Pioneer Press Publishing Co., 1889.

Westerman, Gwen, and Bruce White. *Mni Sota Makoce: The Land of the Dakota.* St. Paul: Minnesota Historical Society Press, 2012.

White, Bruce. "A Dakota Invitation to Coldwater Spring in 1820." MinnesotaHistory.net (blog), December 9, 2012.

White, Bruce, and Alan R. Woolworth. *Oheyawhe or Pilot Knob: Preliminary Summary of the Evidence.* St. Paul, MN: Turnstone Historical Research, January 3, 2003.

Wilson, Angela Cavender. "Grandmother to Granddaughter: Generations of Oral History in a Dakota Family." *American Indian Quarterly* 20, no. 1 (Winter 1996): 7–13.

Wilson, Cynthia. "Hickman, Robert T. (1831–1900)." Blackpast.org. http://www.blackpast.org/aah/hickman-robert-t-1831-1900.

Wilson, Waziyatawin Angela, ed. *In the Footsteps of Our Ancestors: The Dakota Commemorative Marches of the 21st Century.* St. Paul, MN: Living Justice Press, 2006.

Wingerd, Mary. *North Country: The Making of Minnesota.* Minneapolis: University of Minnesota Press, 2010.

Wolfe, Patrick. *Settler Colonialism and the Transformation of Anthropology: The Politics and Poetics of an Ethnographic Event.* New York: Continuum, 1999.

Woolworth, Alan, and Nancy Woolworth. "Carver: Little Cave, Big History." [National Speleological Society,] *NSS News* 38, no. 3 (March 1980): 52–55.

Woolworth, Alan R. Papers. Manuscript Collection, Minnesota Historical Society, St. Paul.

WPA Writer's Project. Slave Narratives. "Hickman, Rev. Robert Thomas." http://arch.law.wustl.edu/Staff/Taylor/SLAVES/hickman.htm.

Index

Italicized page numbers indicate a photo, illustration, or its caption.

Photo Credits

Cover details, left to right: Harriet Scott, 1857; Twenty-First Infantry Band, ca. 1900; Japanese American translators, 1945; Flag Day ceremony, 1944—all Minnesota Historical Society; Joe Perez canoeing at Bdote, 2016—Jon Lurie.

Minnesota Historical Society: cover and page 1, "Mississippi River at Fort Snelling," by an anonymous painter, ca. 1851; pages 2, 9 top and bottom, 10, 11 left (170.52.1.1) and lower right (356.256.8), 13, 14, 17 (8303.2), 18 (001717415), 21 top and bottom, 23, 24 bottom, 25, 28, 32, 34, 36 top and bottom, 42, 43, 49, 51, 55, 56 top and bottom, 57 (detail of "Village of Kaposia," p. 43), 61, 62, 63, 64, 65, 66–67, 69, 70 top and bottom, 73, 74 (Fort Snelling Map Collection), 75, 76, 78, 79, 81, 82, 80, 84, 86, 92 top (Historic Fort Snelling staff)

Nat Case, INCase, LLC: page 7

Matt Schmitt: pages 8, 11 upper right, 22, 26–27, 68, 89, 93, 94–95, 96–97

Library of Congress: page 24 top [Papers of Henry R. Schoolcraft, 1782–1878, "Geological Mineralogical Journal," p. 50 (microfilm M296, reel 48), MNHS, scan courtesy of Michelle Terrell, Two Pines Resource Group, LLC, Shafer, MN]

Fort Winnebago Surgeon's Quarters Historic Site: page 30 (photo by Paul M. Nelson)

Judy Gilats: page 52

Charles C. Royce, *Indian Land Cessions in the United States,* Part 2 of the Eighteenth Annual Report of the Bureau of American Ethnology to the Secretary of the Smithsonian Institution, 1896–97 (Washington, DC: Government Printing Office, 1899): page 48

Ken Epstein: page 54

Mike Patrick: pages 84–85

Peter DeCarlo: pages 90–91

© Brady Willette/Willette Photography, Inc.: page 92 bottom

mnhspress.org

Minnesota Historical Society Press is a member of the Association of University Presses.

Manufactured in the United States of America

10 9 8 7 6 5 4 3 2

∞ The paper used in this publication meets the minimum requirements of the American National Standard for Information Sciences— Permanence for Printed Library Materials, ANSI Z39.48-1984.

International Standard Book Number
ISBN: 978-1-68134-171-2 (paper)

Library of Congress Control Number: 2020933113
Library of Congress Cataloging-in-Publication Data
Names: DeCarlo, Peter, 1988– author.
Title: Fort Snelling at Bdote : a brief history / Peter DeCarlo.
Description: Saint Paul, MN : Minnesota Historical Society Press, [2016] |
Includes bibliographical references.
Identifiers: LCCN 2016047351 | ISBN 9781681340227 (pbk. : alk. paper)
Subjects: LCSH: Fort Snelling (Minn.)—History. | Bdote (Minn.)—History. |
Dakota Indians—Minnesota—History—19th century. | Dakota Indians—
Government relations—History. | Indians, Treatment of—Minnesota—History.
Classification: LCC F614.F7 D43 2016 | DDC 977.6/57—dc23
LC record available at https://lccn.loc.gov/2016047351

Fort Snelling at Bdote was designed and set in type by Judy Gilats.